BABYLON
POST

BABYLON POST

And Other Uncommon Tales from Jeremiah

ROB ALLOWAY

REGENT COLLEGE PUBLISHING
Vancouver, British Columbia

Published 2005 by Regent College Publishing
5800 University Boulevard, Vancouver, BC V6T 2E4 Canada
www.regentpublishing.com

Views expressed in works published by Regent College Publishing are
those of the author and do not necessarily represent the official position of
Regent College <www.regent-college.edu>.

Cover: "Jeremiah," by Gustav Doré.

Library and Archives Canada Cataloguing in Publication Data

Alloway, Robert Raymer
    Babylon post : and other uncommon tales from Jeremiah / Rob
Alloway.

    Includes bibliographical references.
    ISBN 1-57383-225-1

    1. Bible stories, English—O.T. Jeremiah. I. Title.

BS580.J4A44 2005   224'.209505   C2004-905708-1

CONTENTS

1. ELNATHAN 9

2. SHAHEENA 53

3. SAVING JEREMIAH 93

4. THE QUEEN OF HEAVEN 135

5. BABYLON POST 175

ELNATHAN

Some men think of women as they lie on their beds waiting for sleep—sleek, supple young women with flat bellies and smooth skin—the nymphs of youth. I think of blood, Uriah's[1] blood. Its first touch is still warm on my hand and forearm. As I killed him the downward thrust of my short sword into his exposed neck began an eruption of blood that gushed up, splashing onto my hand.

Was I right in killing him? True he was a *nabi*—one of those strange, aloof prophet types that uttered oracles in the name of our God, Yahweh. Uriah promised only our destruction and captivity when hope and confidence were the oracles we needed from our *nabis* during those last turbulent years. But Uriah offered no encouragement. He wreaked havoc on the morale of my troops. How can you stir your men to fight with a holy man ranting that your own God is plotting your downfall? I did not believe he was a loyal Jew. The king ordered him hunted down and killed. God appoints our kings. Uriah at best was a misguided zealot and at worst a traitor in the pay of our enemies. That is the bald essence of my defence.

Why then does Uriah's blood steal into my mind all these years later? Perhaps he was my Passover lamb. Salvation is rarely cheap.

My name is Elnathan.[2] To the chroniclers, I was little more than a name on a list of toadies to the king. Theirs is only the hurried perspective that comes with writing the great epic. They did not know the whole story. Otherwise I would have been given more honour. One thing is sure. I was not a toady.

I got involved, I suppose, only because my daughter was beautiful. She was not beautiful in the chaste, pure sort of spirit that all fathers yearn for. Nehushta had the other kind of beauty, the kind that catches a man's breath and loins, so that he thinks of nothing except how her smooth, firm flesh, curved like moving water, will feel beneath him. I did not see—or chose not to see—her in this way. What father would? But Jehoiakim, our future king, saw her in that light.

He visited our modest garrison town, Lachish, when he was eighteen. I was the chief commander, serving on behalf of my father, Acbor, who was a senior advisor to King Josiah at court. The Assyrians had burnt Lachish sixty years earlier while en route to attack Jerusalem. Jerusalem had withstood the Assyrians only long enough to sue for peace. The terms involved heavy tribute. But the Assyrians had now left our lands. Josiah, as part of his ambitious plans to reclaim all of our former territory and grandeur, had re-established Lachish as the main fortification on his southern flank.

The constraints of our elaborate double-walled entrance only served to irritate Jehoiakim. People entering our city had to first enter from the south, then double back between the two walls to where the inner gate was located. I watched him discreetly as he passed through the southern gate of the outer wall. Jerusalem was only sixty miles away but I could see, even from a distance, the heavy lather hanging in a white gelatinous beard from his horse's mouth. There was no cause for such abuse. Not even bad horsemanship could excuse it. Hurrying north through the town, I was in time to greet him as he entered the final gate positioned in the north section of our inner wall. Why he had come, I did not know. Probably part of some grand tour, either at the command of his father or for his own private interests. For certain, it was a chance to see and be seen, and neither would hurt him if he succeeded his father. He was eldest of Josiah's three sons—probably my next king, although the eldest did not always get the nod. It was prudent to be cordial.

"Welcome, son of Josiah, King of Judah. Your troops are grateful for this royal inspection and your presence brings honour to Lachish and all who serve the king within her walls."

"I need to piss," he replied. He got quickly off his mount and handed me the reins as if I were a stable boy. The insult was brief; someone came and seamlessly took the reins from me.

"Our prince will find a suitable place just inside the stable entrance ahead," I answered, catching up with him. Fortunately he had begun striding off in the right general direction. I let him go ahead of me and stood politely on the courtyard side of the stable doorway, listening to his water fall heavily into the straw strewn inside. His companions—about six of them—had all dismounted but hung back. *A bad beginning*, I thought as he re-emerged into the sunlight.

"The guard is assembled for your review," I ventured, moving my head ever so slightly in the direction of the rows of foot soldiers and archers who stood in formation at the far end of the square.

"I'll nod to them on my way to your chambers," he replied. "They told me it would be hot, but today's sun is beyond endurance." It was a day like any other in our country—no hotter than normal. Except if you'd been drinking along the way.

"The men will be grateful for your consideration of them," I said. It was a deliberate twisting of what he had meant. "They will be glad to be dismissed without delay."

Jehoiakim, if he realized what I'd done, only grunted. I moved with him past the file of troops, doing what I could to strengthen the impression that he was genuinely interested in their review. He wasn't, and I could see on the faces of my men that they felt insulted. They had been in parade formation for most of the morning, waiting for Jehoiakim's arrival. They deserved better.

That afternoon he did consent to walk the outer wall with me. To the west was the Shephelah plain. It was good flat land, ideal for wheat and barley. It was also good for chariots and supply wagons. Always the armies arrived from that direction and had ever since we began defending these lands five hundred years ago, when our twelve tribes had first arrived from Egypt. Eastward, the hill country started quite abruptly. The hills were steep but not high, and offered good grazing on their slopes. They formed a natural obstacle to anyone trying to march on Jerusalem. The roads through them were narrow serpentine threads, stretching an army into a long, thin vulnerable train.

"Do you think Lachish could ever be taken again?" Jehoiakim asked.

"Yes," I replied evenly. I had in mind to begin my petition for more troops, hoping he would carry a favourable recommendation back to his father.

"How?" he asked. "Your walls are thick—almost twenty feet at the base. And besides, you have two of them."

"It would not be easy," I admitted, "and if it came, I suppose it would be the Egyptians this time."

"Why do you say that?" His tone had become more pointed, even inquisitional. I realized I had strayed from a military assessment to a political one. It was not my domain.

"I hear news through my father that the Assyrians continue to focus on their problems far to the north. Their citizens at Babylon give them trouble and the public reports are that there is open war." I laid just enough stress on the word "public" so that there could be no question but that I was reciting common news. "Our Philistine neighbours have no quarrel with us at present and lack the siege equipment required for our fortifications. Who else would challenge your father's independence other than the Egyptians?"

"What do you know of the Egyptians?"

"It is a large country," I ventured. "The Assyrians have retreated from it as they have from our own lands, and the Egyptians have no difficulty in amassing whatever military strength they desire. Besides, it is level ground between them and us and easy enough for the supply wagons to keep an army in the field. Beyond that I hear only the same talk that Jerusalem hears; the usual gossip from the caravaners. At the moment trade is good and flows unmolested, but I understand that your father believes the Egyptians are not to be trusted."

"My father holds many strong beliefs," Jehoiakim said smugly, "and some of them are quite misguided."

I said nothing more on the subject and retreated to the safer problems of rations, water storage, the range of our patrols and other military details. Jehoiakim quickly lost interest. He was not stupid, I concluded. At eighteen, he had all the impetuousness expected of his age, amplified by his father's stubbornness. *But he lacks grace*, I thought. Already I could see the meanness that comes from habitually satisfying your every whim.

As Lachish's senior official, I entertained him and his companions. He stayed only one night. Nehushta led a small group of girls in a dance after the evening meal. Jehoiakim sat at a low table, not once taking his rapacious, reptilian eyes from my daughter. There was something repulsive about him even at table. The more he drank, the less frequently he bothered to wipe his mouth and beard. As the room grew hotter I noticed that his nose had started to run so that, in the flicker of the lamps it looked like there were small jewels dangling from the entrance of each nostril. They would disappear from time to time, as he wiped at them, only to form again. It was not pleasant to think what kind of man he could grow into if he had absolute rule. I sat at his side and watched him devour each morsel that Nehushta threw his way.

Who was this woman with the wide hips and salacious smile wearing the stolen face of my daughter? Shame coloured my cheeks as brightly as the red with which Nehushta had painted her lips. I said nothing to her. What was there to say that would not have been years too late? And if Jehoiakim wasn't the most sensitive of suitors, at least he offered a way out of the cultural impoverishment of a garrison town.

It was no surprise when, less than two weeks later, a court official visited me with the news that the prince intended my daughter as his wife. The news was delivered in the cold, efficient tones of a man who was irritated that even the minimal niceties of a perfunctory conversation with the girl's father had to be endured. It would have been insulting if I had thought it was personal. What Jehoiakim wanted, he took. I wondered what conversations had been exchanged between Josiah and my own father and whether this marriage would be useful to my father's position at court. I wasn't sure. The public acrimony surrounding Josiah's own two marriages did nothing except fuel the fires of court intrigue and gossip. It was not air I cared to breathe.

I suppose I should have been glad my daughter would have the public status of royalty-in-waiting. In truth, it was a union of such unrestrained carnal appetite that I was ashamed. Less than one month later I became father-in-law to prince Jehoiakim, king-in-waiting for the throne of David at Jerusalem—if his luck held. I was not fooled by my new status, knowing full well I was little more than a bit of accidental accretion, stuck on the train of my daughter's sexual accomplishments. In my more insecure moments, I imagined people looking at me with a kind of lewd contempt that I now held modest influence only because of my daughter's breasts. I longed for the clean demands of a garrison outpost, where your commands were simple and delivered in writing.

My wife and I were given quarters within the royal chambers. Lachish was only sixty miles away and I continued to supervise its

although relying more on Hoshaiah,[3] my most experienced
junior officer. Jerusalem's size and population—twenty-five thousand
people—was ten times the size of Lachish. It was not its size that
unsettled me. It was the politics I could not stomach.

As long as Josiah was on the throne life was good. Those were
heady times for our little nation that had been under the Assyrian thumb
for almost seventy years. But for the past twenty years now, at the other
end of the huge Fertile Crescent—a thousand miles away measured
by the caravan routes—the Babylonians had been in open revolt. And
they'd been winning. Together with their northern neighbours, the
Medes, they'd steadily hacked away at the eastern half of the Assyrian
Empire. Ninevah, the Assyrian ancient capital, had been taken two
years before and the Assyrians were now massed around a city called
Carchemish. So far they had lost about half of their former lands.

The worse things got for the Assyrians, the better they got for us.
It had been almost ten years since we'd last seen any Assyrian troops,
and those had been marching quickly back to defend the eastern flank.
For us it was like springtime after a long, cruel winter and we thought
it would last forever.

Josiah was a good king. My father certainly respected him, and my
father was past the age when he held his tongue against fools.

"Headstrong, but pure," he told me one day. "Doesn't listen to
his military advisors very well, but he's not yet been in battle. He's a
fanatic about following Yahweh though, so he listens to the priests."

"Is he exclusive in his worship then?" I asked.

"Ever since he found the old law books of Moses. They were sealed
up behind a false wall in the temple. The architects couldn't account
for about ten feet of space when they were drawing the plans for the
refurbishment, so we started nosing about. Found a whole library, we
did. I was sent to consult Huldah the prophetess."[4]

"He takes it all seriously then?" I had wondered what lay behind
the latest round of orders I'd been carrying out. I'd just come back from
a month's assignment to the north of Jerusalem, not my usual patrol.
Part of our detachment had been seconded and I'd gone with them.

"You won't recognize Jerusalem, Son. Seven temples destroyed and
nineteen altars to other gods smashed. Everything Manasseh spent a
lifetime commissioning has been burned or trashed by his grandson,

Josiah. We've had about a hundred priests and attendants executed. Some we let just vanish. Not the male prostitutes though. Even tore down their quarters."[5]

"Well, at least he's consistent," I answered. We've been doing pretty much the same thing up country, right up to Samaria.

"Whores in the service of false gods—that's what Josiah charged them with. Ishtar, Molech, Baal or Chemosh—it didn't matter which temple employed them, or how junior their duties, Josiah ordered them killed."

"What is the news from Lachish?" I asked. I knew it had a small shrine to Asherah and a few of the town merchants made idols. It was too newly built to have anything substantial. My orders made more sense when I thought about it more. Better that troops from a different area moved in and did the dirty work. Some of the priests, and more to the point, priestesses, would be all too familiar friends of the soldiers. The cult of Ishtar, in particular, maintained a bevy of prostitutes. It was part of the liturgy. Ishtar was, after all, the patron goddess of fertility.

"The shrine is gone. One merchant had his stall smashed and we haven't seen the other one who traded in idols," my father answered.

"What is the news from the north?" he asked in return.

I thought about the past month. Our pattern hadn't changed much from town to town. Between thirty and fifty mounted troops would charge through the town gates, pounding hard for the biggest temple we could see. There would be no advance notice. A few of the luckier priests, those on duty, would rush out at the sound of our horses and be run through cleanly. Others would emerge from side doors, hoping to escape, but we would always be waiting for them. Occasionally there would be mad-dash chases through the town, market stalls upturned, awnings pulled down. The angry shouts of merchants covered some of the cries from killings that were not so clean. It's hard to kill a man cleanly from astride a horse in a tightly packed city street. You can't swing your sword properly—it's all forward thrust and you have to avoid civilians. It often takes several stabs before the man falls. Then, if he's still moving, you have to dismount for the final short stroke of certainty.

In every town it was much the same. If it was walled, we got most of the priests and temple servants while they were still inside the town.

If the town was open, we'd have to chase some of them up into the hills. It was a diversion for my men, but it certainly wasn't battle. The orders had been clear: if the temple wasn't in the service of Yahweh we were to kill the priests and burn their bodies on their own god's altar before torching or smashing everything. The ashes of what we burned were to be scattered—nothing left but the black stain of soot. By order of Josiah, who served only Yahweh.

I wondered how best to answer my father, what he was looking for. He'd heard enough military reports to make all but the main facts unnecessary.

"Uneventful," I replied at last. "We lost one man— his horse threw him just as he was passing through a gate and he hit his head on the stones. Stupid accident. No opposition of course. We never stayed in one place long enough for the town councils to whine about the damages to their markets. I don't know the mood of the people, if that is what you're asking." After a pause I added, "Puzzled, if I had to pick a word."

"That won't last long," replied my father. "Josiah is sending heralds out shortly to proclaim the biggest celebration since Solomon. The Feast of the Passover is just two months away and Jerusalem will host it. Josiah has proclaimed that it will be celebrated at the original temple. The priests of Yahweh are ecstatic, of course. And politically, it's pure brilliance."

"Passover? Here at Jerusalem? Only here?"

My father chuckled. He could see that I was hurriedly trying to assess the logistical implications of the event. By any criteria, it would be a huge undertaking.

"All in accordance with the instructions of Moses," my father answered. "Josiah has gone so far as to close all other Yahweh temples except Jerusalem."

"So much for local independence," I muttered. Then, more loudly, "The court council approves of all this?"

"Wholeheartedly. It's like spring cleaning on a grand scale. Everything foreign is expunged, including the whole panoply of gods who have commanded our allegiance. For the first time in living memory, Judah is independent. Why should we not return to the one

God who is truly and exclusively our own? It's never enough just to tear down. You have to give the people something else to rally around."

I shrugged. Religion and the throne were inseparable. If the king declared that no other god was to be acknowledged save Yahweh, no other justification was needed—or expected, for that matter. I wondered privately at all the adjustments to our way of life that would be set in play. The idea of only one God would take some getting used to. It wasn't just the disruption to our economic affairs. These were precarious times; you tried to be on good terms with everyone in the heavens and on earth. But the prospect of a national feast, paid for by the court, was a refreshing change, exciting even. I could picture the kind of pilgrimage it would instigate.

Jerusalem bulged like the stomach of an ox let loose in the granary—bloated and distended with the crowd of pilgrims responding to Josiah's summons. Overnight our population trebled. People camped and squatted everywhere and when the streets could finally hold no more, the crowd spilled out our gates like rolls of brightly coloured flab over a fat man's girdle.

The smell of roasted meat was everywhere. Josiah had donated more than thirty thousand animals from his herds. All were killed on the one altar and then hurriedly carted away to the various stations set up to dress out the carcasses. The Levites—the exclusive priests for Yahweh—worked in shifts of not more than two hours. The pace of slaughter was extraordinary. I watched as one crew left the main altar, staggering off with blood-soaked tunics. It was all being done as closely to the code of Moses as was possible. On that, Josiah's instructions were inviolate. At most street corners large open braziers had been set up and the meat—the portions not burned in sacrifice or reserved for the Levites—was relayed to these stations for cooking. Other officials[6] in the city had opened their own storehouses and added grain, oil, spices and dried fruits to our national, holy orgy.

I first saw Uriah at the feast. It was an event that brought out every prophet, every entertainer, every huckster, thief and charlatan; all the parasites that live off large crowds no matter why they are gathered.

There was lots of time to fill—the whole city, meat juice running down our collective chin—hunched down to seven days of free food.

Uriah was tall, awkwardly built, with bones that stuck out. He reminded me of an ugly horse I had once owned. He seemed well known and someone told me that he'd taught for a while at the Tablet school. He had taken up a station by the corner of a large house, where he stood on the plinth of the corner pillar.

"Enjoying the Passover are you?" he began. "Getting your fill of lamb and other choice morsels? Think this is a pretty good way of showing your loyalty to Yahweh—by outeating each other at the royal trough?"

Someone called back—these public oratories were rarely one sided—"Uriah, you should be happy for once. Our whole country is now devoted to Yahweh. Why do you seek to make our meal sour within our stomachs?" There was a low, relaxed laugh. Then someone else called out. "Uriah is like the gas that comes after the meal—unavoidable but it passes." Even Uriah smiled at that crack.

"Do you think Yahweh is taken in by all your celebrations? You've all come slinking back to his temple to renew your vows, and make up for a whole lifetime of service at other shrines? Good loyal Jews are you?"

"It's what Moses commanded," someone shouted. "And he was the greatest *nabi* ever—are you greater than he was, Uriah? Besides, there is nowhere else to worship."

"You speak of Moses and his instructions—as if the details of whether the lambs you eat were cut with their heads facing north or east are of interest to Yahweh. Do you want to hear the words of Yahweh for this day?" Uriah did not give anyone a chance to answer, but launched ahead.

"Thus says Yahweh: 'Go ahead and offer sacrifices; add to them; eat the meat and deceive yourself that this is enough. When I brought your forefathers out of the land of Egypt, I did not just instruct them in the ways of sacrifice and burnt offerings. I gave them this command: Obey me! Follow only me and the ways I have established for you. And you have not listened. You circumcise your loins easily enough, but your hearts are still a'whoring. You persist in worshipping other gods; you pervert justice; truth has gone out from your loins. The fatherless and the alien are considered lawful prey in this land; you shed innocent blood and sleep with your neighbours' wives. And then you come and stand here in my holy city, with the juices of a sacrifice that is not even your own swishing about your mouths and say, "We are safe."'"

"Do you think that just because the Assyrians have left us alone for a little while we are safe? Do you think God is going to be mocked forever by his own people and not bring judgment crashing down on your heads? I tell you the truth—Yahweh's truth: this city and all who live in it will perish. For Yahweh's judgment cannot be escaped."[7]

There was more, but I moved on. He had a point about the sudden public allegiance to the God of our ancestors. I suspected it was a superficial change. Baal and Ishtar were rooted deep in this land. Those were the gods that had welcomed us when we arrived. Yahweh was our travelling god. Certainly, nothing I'd seen in my patrols made me think we'd embraced some new standard of civic morality. But then justice had always been a little rougher on the frontiers—which in our country meant most everywhere except Jerusalem.

Nabis are exclusive to Yahweh worship. The tradition went back to Moses, and so we accepted them, suffering them like an ugly family relic we could not throw away, yet displayed with fierce pride to the sundry visitors that came to visit.

It was a vocation that mixed public oratory, historical memory and current events into salty brine, and then ladled it into our ears as the authoritative voice of Yahweh. Some held the vocation in high regard, diligently seeking the mind of Yahweh; some milked the office—offering pleasing oracles that would return a good purse. Uriah's kind were like a strain of angry hornets that would not leave our land, a constant, irritating buzz in our ears, telling us that whatever we were doing at that particular moment was the wrong thing. Unending harassment: "Thus says Yahweh. Thus says the God of Moses. Thus says the God who gave you this land, gave you this holy city, who dwells in his holy temple, who watches over the throne of David . . ." They uttered the prologues like a public badge of office, and because of it they were allowed more latitude in what they said. Still, even for them, there were lines they could not cross—not if they wanted to stay alive.

I joined the royal family for only one of their evening feast meals. It was a lavish affair, solemn, but not even the rituals of the Passover could expunge the yeast of dysfunction that permeated the royal household. Entrenched hostility smouldered permanently among its members. Josiah may have been king of Judah, but within his own household, dysfunction reigned supreme.

On either side of Josiah sat his two wives. Zebidah, Jehoiakim's mother, had the preferred seat, to the right of the king. She was his first wife and Jehoiakim had been born almost immediately after their marriage. Zebidah had gone to fat quickly afterward. Josiah was fourteen at the time of the first marriage. It probably came as a huge disappointment to discover that women aren't always the same after childbirth.

Josiah had married his second wife, Hamutal, two years later, some said because he resented the strictures that childbearing placed on his sexual proclivity. Hamutal was quite careful with her looks and had escaped the ravages of childbirth while delivering her two sons, Jehoahaz and Zedekiah. The two women never spoke to each other in public, although palace rumour said their private exchanges could sound like two vultures shrieking over the same dead meat.

Platters began to move up and down the table and cautious conversation about the events of the week commenced. I watched as Nehushta played the dutiful daughter-in-law to Josiah. She had dressed discreetly for the meal but even the modest robe did not conceal her still-firm body. The birth of my grandson, Jehoiachin, had left her charms intact. *God help my daughter if she ever runs to fat like Zebidah*, I thought. I did not think Jehoiakim's affections for her were deeply rooted.

Finally, after about an hour, when the trivial details of the feast had been exhausted, Hamutal steered the conversation into more serious talk.

"What is the news of Carchemish?" she asked Josiah loudly enough to quiet the chatter.

"My scouts say most of the Assyrian army has dug in. They are determined to make a stand. It is only a question of when Nebuchadnezzar begins his assault."

"Will it be this year, do you think?" It was Jehoahaz, younger half-brother to Jehoiakim by two years. The two brothers got along about as well as their mothers.

"No, I do not think so," Josiah answered. "Probably next year though. Time works against Nebuchadnezzar in this campaign. But Carchemish is five hundred miles away from Babylon and it will take at least until spring for Nebuchadnezzar to bring up enough provisions and siege machinery to even hope to succeed.

"And what will be the outcome, Father?" Jehoiakim asked.

"Assyria is finished."

"That will be sweet news when my ears receive it," said Hamutal. "May it be done to them as they have done to others."

"Twice over," joined in someone else and a general stir of approval rippled round the room.

"And when Nebuchadnezzar is finished at Carchemish, will his army return meekly to Babylon?" Jehoiakim's voice had just a tinge of challenge in it.

This was not lost on Josiah, who replied, "Babylonians are both civilized and reasonable. They have not been the aggressors in this piece but, like us, are only throwing off the yoke of oppression."

"And tribute," added Jehoahaz. He had meant the remark to be both humorous and insightful, but he had this nervous habit of grinning foolishly, which made whatever he said hard to take seriously. He was one of those "anxious to please at all costs" types—genuinely superficial. Still, he was the preferred son at court over Jehoiakim, in part because he was complaisant with the council of advisors that stood around the throne.

"So you think we can continue to enjoy our independence then?" Jehoiakim asked. "You have received some assurances from the Babylonian court of their intentions?"

"We are a small nation," said Josiah testily, "but watched over by a mighty God. You forget what feast you eat this night. Josiah's temper was quickly stirred and was as virulent as some of his other passions.

"It's an unusual strategy for dealing with foreign nations who cast a long shadow—trusting in an unseen God." Jehoiakim's tone was acidly neutral.

21

"A strategy which so far seems to be working, I would judge," answered Josiah. "I am unaware of any foreign troops on Jewish soil at present."

Jehoiakim, sensing the threatening signals from his father, elected not to push the discussion. "Well said, Father, well said." His tone conceded the conversation to Josiah. The table relaxed and conversation drifted to other matters.

It was late when a servant entered my sleeping chambers with a whispered message that Jehoiakim wished to see me. Now. He was nervous lest I refuse. Jehoiakim was known to abuse his menials. Yet he knew full well, as did I, that this was not a royal summons and I was within my rights to decline.

I didn't decline, of course. Irritating my son-in-law and future king served no purpose.

"Thank you for coming," said Jehoiakim. "You did not have to." His civility and candour caught me off guard. His speech was clear, despite the smell of wine on his breath.

"Yours is to command," I replied.

"Not yet," Jehoiakim said with a small grin. I said nothing, just waited.

Finally, he spoke. "There are certain communications of a private nature I require delivered. The usual avenues are not . . . convenient to me, and I need someone with both loyalty and discretion."

"King's business?" I asked.

"Royal business," he replied.

Another silence.

"To whom are the letters being sent?" I asked.

"There is a prince at Pharaoh's court in Egypt. His name is Neco. He will succeed his father shortly. He is already publicly anointed. There are no secrets there."

Not there, I thought, *but here for sure.*

Jehoiakim continued in a measured voice. "He and I have established a certain friendship. We exchange confidences so as to be accurately informed about our respective affairs."

A hundred thoughts flashed through my head like a flock of arrows all let loose at the same time. Was this an act of treason? How much did Josiah already know about his son's foreign relations? Should I refuse?

22

Could I refuse? How much did I want to know about this clandestine request? This final thought registered within me, and running through a host of outcomes — none of them good for me—I decided to do it. *Leave the politics to others. Delivering letters, by itself, is not an act of treason.*

"It is a small service for me to provide the royal household," I said at last. "Where are the letters?"

Jehoiakim handed over several sealed papyri. The broad sheets of flattened reed, written with wide margins, had been folded several times in one direction. The sides were then brought into the centre. Where they touched, a liberal amount of wax had been applied in which I could see the imprint of his scribe's signet ring. For added strength each letter had been secured with thin cord. The result was a tamper-proof parcel about the thickness of my finger joint and less than a foot long.

"Am I to wait for a reply?" I asked.

"Yes."

"It will be unwise for me to stay, even a night. A few hours would be preferred. Nothing is gained from loitering."

"I will add another note to that effect," said Jehoiakim. "It will be delivered to you before dawn."

There was another silence as we studied each other carefully, reading for the unspoken message.

Don't think I'm afraid of you, was what I wanted him to see in my face.

Respect my power, if not me, was what I saw in his.

———

I took command of about thirty men under the guise of an extended tour of our southern lands. It was within my purview. By convention, Josiah's jurisdiction stopped at the Brook of Egypt, the Wadi el Arish, which was one full day's ride south of Lachish. Memphis was another two hundred miles away. It was there I would find Neco, no doubt embroiled in his own court stratagems. How I hated the politics. Past the brook of Egypt, I took only two men with me and we splashed quietly over the border, each trailing a spare mount. One of my men spoke a little Egyptian. We kept our uniforms on for the first half of the journey—past the city of Migdol, right to where the Nile delta started in earnest.

"We'll shift to civilian clothes here," I said, about the middle of our second day. And on we rode toward the Egyptian capital, down into the bowels of Egypt. We were just three more well-equipped foreigners going about some urgent commercial matter. There were lots of Jews in Egypt—small communities at On, Thebes and even Elphantine, some three hundred miles south of Memphis. Three more Jews on the road wouldn't excite much comment. Was I wrong to have concealed the insignia of Josiah, which would have established me as a legitimate envoy on a state mission? My conscience did not trouble me overly. Before I left, I had told my father about my mission. Let the council deal with it if they wanted to wade into Jehoiakim's affairs.

In the end, what I thought did not matter. Nothing did. Six months later Josiah was dead from an Egyptian arrow in his back. The irony was that Jehoiakim's intrigues, whatever they were or were not, had nothing to do with it. Neco, having succeeded his father, made a shrewd bet on the war in the north and sent troops to help the Assyrians keep the Babylonians at bay. It meant sending a huge convoy seven hundred miles north to the vicinity of Carchemish, where the Assyrians had taken a stand. It was a farsighted strategy. If the Babylonians could be turned back, or at least stopped, before they crossed the Euphrates then Egypt would have unfettered control of the whole western arm of the Fertile Crescent. They were the lands of the Edomites, the Philistines, the seaport of Tyre, the Syrians, and us. In the meantime, Assyria, in a much humbled condition, would be retained as a chained yard dog, hunched on the most northern part of Egypt's interests, barking a first alert if Nebuchadnezzar came sniffing for the spoils of Palestine.

For it to work, Neco had to march one hundred and fifty thousand troops, chariots, supply wagons, archers and mounted units across the Sinai desert, over the Brook of Egypt and northward up the coastal plain of the Great Sea. All he sought from Josiah was safe passage through Judah's territory. He even went so far as to deliver a flattering petition for safe conduct, promising to pay a reasonable head tax for the inconvenience.

Josiah refused. Against the advice of the court, my father included, Josiah gathered the military, swelled its ranks with enthusiastic volunteers and rode to intercept Neco's army. It took on the fervour of a holy crusade. Yahweh would ride with them. No foreign troops on Jewish soil!

To the north of Jerusalem the coastal plain is interrupted by the Carmel mountain range. Only the Megiddo pass is large enough for an army to use, and even then it is vulnerable until it can regroup on the open plains that start again quite quickly just north of the mountains. Josiah had hoped to ride north in time to attack while the bulk of Neco's troops were still making their way through the pass. We were two days late. What confronted us was a disciplined wall of Egyptian charioteers. Our losses were horrific and Josiah's body was paraded home through a stunned and silent countryside.

Why did Josiah commit to such a reckless course? Was it just the arrogance of youth intoxicated by our recent freedoms? Or did Josiah see himself as Yahweh's divine agent, meting out the promised retribution[8] for almost a century of Assyrian atrocities against our people? If that were the case, then Egypt could not be allowed to give aid to our former masters. Yahweh had decreed their punishment.

Jehoahaz was crowned king in a quick and muted ceremony. Suprisingly Jehoiakim did not protest. I thought it strange at the time. He was the eldest son and had a legitimate claim despite being unpopular. For three months we lived on the edge of a monstrous thunderstorm that raged to our north. Directly overhead the sun shone brightly enough. But one gaze at the oily grey maelstrom to the north and a clammy cold pierced our illusionary safety.

Finally the storm moved our way. It came in the form of two hundred Egyptians, mounted troops in full ceremonial dress. A seasoned old campaigner—who, since he could not murder us all directly, took vicarious glee in butchering our language—led them. He did not even dismount but rode his horse up onto the first broad terrace that fronted the public palace entrance.

"It pleases Neco, Pharaoh of Egypt, to grant you his protection against the Babylonian vermin whom we have defeated on the plains of Haran. I have been instructed to escort your king"—here he paused and made as if he was peering at a scrap of papyrus in his hand—"Je-ho-a-ha-zz," reading out each syllable as if astonished that such a word could exist. "Your king, Je-ho-a-ha-zz," he repeated the joke into the air, "is to meet with Neco's appointed satraps for this region, who are stationed at Riblah."

By the time he finished, the back edge of the terrace was packed with officials, who had spilled out of the palace interior. Jehoahaz, to his credit, came forward.

"May it please Neco to hear that I will follow you shortly and confer with his officials."

"It will please Neco more to hear that you came with us—now."

An older councillor stepped forward. Shaphan was his name. "Jehoahaz, our king," he deliberately emphasized the word, "is just newly anointed. There are certain pressing matters requiring his wisdom here."

The Egyptian glanced down at his papyrus scrap again, then said, "He has a brother, Jehoiakim, who will take his place."

And in less than half an hour, Jehoahaz had ridden out of our gates surrounded by Egyptians, ostensibly for a regional consultation.

It took a *nabi* to ring out loudly the reality of what had happened. Say one thing about the prophetic guild: hearing them is like having cold water sluiced over your head after a hard night in the cups. Jeremiah, a colleague of Uriah's, was the *nabi* who had the insight of the moment and the courage to speak it out. That very evening he mounted the temple steps and shouted into the grey light that invades our city each evening:

"You know the truth. Take out the clothes of mourning you so recently wore to honour Josiah. Put them back on. Find ashes for your face. Weep again, but not for Josiah. He at least sleeps peacefully in honour among his fathers. But weep for him who was exiled this day. Weep bitterly for the king who will die the death of a slave in Egypt.

"And weep also for yourselves. For Jehoahaz is only the first who will be led out from our gates in chains. For thus says Yahweh, the unseen God you do not heed, who you think sleeps through your trysts with other gods that you take like lovers into the couches of your hearts: 'I have rejected you. I have removed Myself from you and will destroy this, my holy city, and all who live in her. Jehoahaz is but the firstfruit of a whole harvest gone to rot.'"[9]

Jeremiah proved right. We never saw Jehoahaz again. *So this is what Jehoiakim has been planning,* I thought. *Except it was supposed to have been his father, Josiah, taken into captivity. His death was a bonus in the scheme. Now, Jehoahaz, his half-brother, is removed as well.*

———

For all the years Jehoiakim ruled us, he never grasped the concept of public duty. To be king was to have been granted some kind of divine franchise to perpetual self-indulgence. And as long as his Egyptian friends received their monthly tribute, there was nothing to be done. It fell to the military regiments to collect the taxes and in light of my past "experience," as Jehoiakim would remind me from time to time with a conspiratorial wink, I would command the deliveries to Memphis. At first there was enough surplus in the land to pay the tax. But the reserves did not last—could not last with Jehoiakim financing his antics. At times I felt I carried the lifeblood of our people down to the altar of Egypt. Maybe real worship of the gods we serve takes place far away from their temple residences. If Jehoiakim had even once protested to Neco that the taxes were too high, if he had even once seemed concerned about the constant grinding down of most everyone who lived beyond Jerusalem, it would not have seemed so humiliating. But he bent his knee willingly, just so long as it didn't touch him.

The years passed. I avoided Jerusalem if I could. My father aged quickly in the new climate at court. Nehushta's pale beautiful skin developed a blotchy rash that would not go away. She had a furtive look in her eyes. Once I saw her with a large, ugly welt on her right cheek. "A careless fall in my chambers," she said. I wondered.

The old guard of councillors, solid men like my father— Shaphan, Hilkiah and Ashaiah—were drifting away, and if they did not actually leave, their influence diminished. The younger crowd who took their place was louder in both dress and speech. It was a dangerous time to be at court and have opinions other than the king's.

The conflict to our north lulled. Nebuchadnezzar had paused to regroup his forces and consolidate his territories. Egypt's control over the western part of the Fertile Crescent was, I judged, tenuous.

She did not garrison our lands the way the Assyrians had before her. Whether she could not spare the troops or took assurances from Jehoiakim's docile submission I was not sure. The military assessment was that another, more decisive conflict between Nebuchadnezzar and the Egyptian/Assyrian coalition was inevitable. In our small world Jehoiakim carried on with the grand illusion that all was well. Those who supported the great lie found favour.

———

When I received the conscription order, I did not act on it. I did not believe it. Instead I rode hard up to Jerusalem that same day. Not for nothing was I the king's father-in-law. The orders were madness itself. They were the products of a besotted, selfish mind that had no concept of prudent rule. They were a debauched cruelty played out on the helpless countryside. They were all that and more. I mentally rehearsed my speech of protest as I rode the sixty miles to Jerusalem. This time my horse arrived foam-flecked. Jehoiakim saw me readily enough.

"Forced labour—slave labour. That's what these orders are," I confronted him. "You want thirty men from every walled town and ten from every village to come to Jerusalem for the construction of your palace renovation. You offer no pay. It's the pyramids all over again." Jehoiakim let me vent. The more I talked, the more he smirked.

"Elnathan, I am merely allowing each village to participate in a grand national monument. The palaces at Memphis are the pride of all Egyptians. Why should our people not have something similar?"

"But to force the labour from them! Why not pay them, or hire the Syrians for this kind of thing? They're noted for it."

A pause. Then, "The royal exchequer must not be squandered foolishly. My orders stand. Be reasonable, father-in-law. What protest you encounter will not endure, especially after the building is complete. Those who work on it will be honoured in their villages."

"You will not rescind the conscription then?" I asked.

"I am within my rights. The order will stand. See that you deliver your allotted workers. I would not have it said that my own family was shy in their duties."

I sought out my father. He was appalled by the orders but had no counsel. "The king's treasury is depleted, if you are wondering why he doesn't pay," he told me. "The timbers we get from Tyre require hard payment. Credit is in short supply just at present. Jehoiakim is intent on building a monument to himself and thinks of nothing else, even if it means making outright slaves of our own people.

"What should I do?" I asked him.

"Am I to counsel treason?" he answered. We stared at each other, shocked that the conversation had so quickly run to its only natural end. Finally, he continued, "My son, it has been discussed among some. But always the alternatives seem no better than what we presently endure. Josiah's third son, Zedekiah, is hardly older than your own grandson. Neither is old enough to rule—they are hardly known. There is no clear coalition among the households or guilds—is civil war better than what we have now? Besides, the Egyptians might take exception to someone killing their vassal, especially one who lives with his lips tethered to their backsides."

My father was right. Better what we had than plunge the country into chaos. So out I went with my detachments and began the sorry task of recruitment. Rounding up the conscripts occasioned my first prayer, although to whom I spoke I was not sure. I named Yahweh. I thought he, being a Jewish god, would at least be more interested than others. *Let me not have to kill anyone.*

No one ever volunteered from the towns. By the time we arrived, some of the more shrewd or cruel villages had already selected their representatives: the stupid, the unliked or just the unlucky ones. It was a good way to rid the community of problem citizens, at least for a time. But usually it was our job to round up the number. There was no resistance, just stiff-backed outrage. I remember one young girl, not yet pubescent, who kicked my leg as I hustled her father out of his hut. Her mother gasped, and her face held a mixture of fear for how I might respond, yet pride in her daughter's spontaneous courage. I endured the insult, knowing it was justified.

Rounding up the conscripts occasioned Uriah's last public oracle. He approached the palace just before the first strong light. You could not really see him, only a tall, indistinct vertical apparition standing on a pile of building stones.

"Jehoiakim," his voice echoed. The usual morning noises of a city rousing itself had not yet started. "Jehoiakim, you who sleep behind those rich, red tapestries. Tell me, Jehoiakim, does it make you a better king than Josiah now that your palace is bigger? Do you mark your measure in the quantity of cedar with which you panel your walls? Do you think it is for your large and elegant windows that you will be remembered?

"It will be for extortion that you are remembered: Jehoiakim, the king who made slaves of his people and made them work without pay. You can think of nothing else except your own vanity. So hear what Yahweh has in store for you, Jehoiakim, for thus says the God who sees everything: 'People will not mourn you. You will have the burial of a donkey—dragged away and thrown outside the gates of Jerusalem.'"[10]

———

"Ignore the oracle. Uriah is not even respected among the other *nabis*. He has no following," the more cogent councillors said.

"Ignore an act of public treason?"

"Protest surely, not treason. It is, after all, their prerogative. These *nabis* always speak in extremes. It is an expected style—a turn of speech only."

"He called me an ass. He said I was not popular. I won't have it," Jehoiakim ranted, gyrating around the room where he was eating his first meal of the day like a yearling testing the confines of his stall.

Finally Ahikam, who served as a kind of prosecutor and legal advocate for the throne, spoke. "Jehoiakim, the royal household has tolerated the occasional prophetic irritation and borne it with the gracious forbearance that befits your status." Shaphan, the chief court secretary in Josiah's time, was Ahikam's father. He and the families who supported him had not yet offered up their reason in a slavish bid for Jehoiakim's favour. Ahikam continued, "A similar outburst by Jeremiah was allowed in the end. Moreover, Jeremiah's oracle was even more abusive. He promised mass exile to Babylon; that Jerusalem would become a refuse site. In short, he promised that Yahweh would visit us with a wrath not seen since the days of Sodom and Gomorrah.[11]

'Shameless prostitution of our hearts'[12] was his more colourful accusation as I recall."

"Yes, I have not forgotten, and were it not for your meddling,[13] he'd be dead too."

"I seek only the welfare of your throne and all who occupy it," said Ahikam evenly. "You rule by the will of Yahweh, who has ordained that the sons of David shall prevail. It is an authority you do well to keep untarnished and unquestioned. It is part of the glue that sticks you to the royal seat. The throne of David does not kill off the prophets of Yahweh, however outlandish their oracles are from time to time. You gnaw away at your own throne if you do."

"Untarnished?" Jehoiakim spluttered. "It is Uriah and the other mongrel dogs like him who chew the legs of David's throne like a bone."

"They speak in the name of Yahweh," said Ahikam, "and, I might add, are bound by their own code. Let his words drift off like a bad odour. And when they do not come to pass, Uriah will be exposed for the charlatan he is. Prophets who deal in lies just to attract attention are not accepted by the guild. His own kind will censor him soon enough."

"He called me an ass," Jehoiakim whined. "I will not allow it." And whirling around to me, he shouted, "Find Uriah and bring him to me."

"As the king commands," I replied.

Ahikam merely shrugged. Others looked everywhere but at each other.

I searched the city, loudly with much public show. I did it with all the energy of a visitor who makes a point of asking for directions at every corner. I sought him diligently. But alas, my noise must have preceded me, for Uriah could not be found. I reported the same to Jehoiakim, stonefaced. The matter had ended and I slipped away to Lachish.

But it did not end. When Jehoiakim summoned me a month later he was almost manic in his glee.

"Uriah is in Egypt." He grinned at me as if this news would be instantly significant.

"Beyond our borders, then."

"He seeks to harm our interests there."

"He seeks to stay alive," I answered.

"He will speak against the tribute. He will claim I am plotting independence."

"So?" I was still not clear where this was going.

"So, he is a fugitive, guilty of treason—an enemy of one throne surely is not to be trusted anywhere. He is a destabilizer. Neco might think he has been sent into his midst deliberately . . . and take offence . . . unless, of course, Uriah is brought back."

The trap sprang shut. The last thing we needed was Egyptian troops garrisoned at Jerusalem.

"It's not as if you've never been to Egypt before," Jehoiakim crooned at me.

"He has a point," my father offered when I sought him out. "Picture the scene if it happened here. A wild-eyed Egyptian shows up sputtering invectives against Neco. It would seem odd if Egyptian troops did not come to fetch him back. Jehoiakim is terrified lest Neco think Uriah has been sent to Egypt."

Ahikam, when I asked him privately, was more blunt. "Uriah has become a high-profile nuisance. Egypt does not wish to be seen harbouring opposition to a vassal king. It is ultimately an attack on their authority, too, since Jehoiakim reigns at their pleasure. This has ceased to be a small matter of an upstart *nabi* who had the temerity to be indiscreet about a few Jewish labourers."

I said nothing, and Ahikam said finally, "I am sorry yours is the sordid task of dealing with this—sorrier still that Jehoiakim will have his way. He is a cruel bastard—hard to believe that Josiah sired him. He is all that Uriah called him and then some." I judged it best to ignore Ahikam's indiscretion. *The pressures at court must be intense,* I thought.

Memphis is already seventy miles inland from the great sea, Elphantine another three hundred. I distracted myself through the days by rehearsing and revising my military assessment. Egypt was mobilizing a new army. The evidence was everywhere. Carts piled high with grain sacks, wagons full of spear shafts cut from the southern forests, or stacked with tanned hides that would become breastplates, shields and belts; the proof of a large mobilization lumbered past us each day.

One rule taught early in military training is this: Never, never make friends with your prisoner.

Uriah led us on a merry chase. The whole Nile delta is barely above sea level and there is no wind. Our sweat built up a sheen of salt on our uniforms. Our skin itched and chafed. The bugs—cruel Egyptian residents—never left us. We traveled on our own meagre rations.

But a fugitive Jew in a foreign country travels without camouflage. We finally caught Uriah at Elphantine, in the middle of the Nile, on an island where the Jews live.

By the time I caught up with him I could have happily fed him to the crocodiles that paddled in silent patrol in the Nile. Egypt was a forbidding land. We did not belong and were reminded of it constantly.

Another hundred miles and Uriah would have been out of Egypt entirely and into the land of the Ethiopians. He tried to bolt even as we cornered him. I hit him in the face with my encased forearm. The force of it split his upper lip badly. After that he came quietly enough. Here was no demented inciter, just a man who had opened his big ungainly mouth at the wrong time. We kept his hands bound to the saddle pommel and led his mount. We were a party of fifteen men, but I am a cautious man. He didn't complain, was almost cheerful although he must have known what awaited him.

One night we bivouacked in the Sinai and we all drew in close to the fire. Deserts are as cold at night as they are hot in the day. I sat next to him and, were it not for the rope around his ankles and wrists, we could have been companions.

"We'll be in Jerusalem within four days, I expect," Uriah ventured.

"We've made good time," I acknowledged.

"Moses took a more scenic route," he said lightly.

"Yes, but forty years? That's enough time to have seen every rock and bush thrice over."

"You forget, he was waiting."

"For what?"

"For a whole generation to die off. They reached our land quickly enough at first and then decided they couldn't conquer it. Yahweh judged them unfit to enter the land. Their children would have that privilege."

"This Yahweh God of yours cares for his people in strange ways," I said.

"God of *ours*," he corrected me. "We'd already been in Egypt for four hundred years. Forty more years wasn't much to his mind, I'm sure."

"Still, for the generation that left their bones in this wilderness—not exactly the Promised Land for them."

We sat facing the fire. Uriah said, "It will not be the first time God has wanted to destroy us and start over. But always he leaves a small seedling—some remnant."

"So you do not recant of your warnings that Jerusalem will fall, and all who live in her will be destroyed?"

"Would that I could. I did not ask for this prescience that plays out in my mind, so clear as if it has already happened. It is my curse I have carried from an early age—even before Tablet school."

"Many *nabis* disagree with you—maybe you are mistaken in your visions of the future." I wondered if he would bend even a little.

"Many speak visions from their own minds, but few have stood in the council of Yahweh. They speak the delusions of their own minds—dreams of distraction, the euphoric projections of what they want to see. It sells well in the streets and at court, but it is not from Yahweh."[14]

As Uriah prattled on through his thick lip, I withdrew into my own, more practical, thoughts. Contemplating the vengeance of an unseen god was a speculation that seemed childish, almost self-indulgent. The condition of our mounts, the quantity of rations, the health of my men—already two could hardly ride from the weakness of fever—it wasn't the things I couldn't see that worried me; it was the things I could. Molech, Baal, Ishtar, Yahweh—they were all just names, and their servants were expendable to our national interests. Temple worship was a diversion, keeping both fear and hysteria from destroying us. Nothing more. And for those who chose that line of work, they would do best to know their purpose. Uriah's rantings were, frankly, boring. But they were also more. They were treasonous. There is no compromising with treason.

We entered the city quietly, Uriah on foot. His bound hands were tethered to a saddle and the lead was deliberately shortened so that he had to run beside the horse with his hands at chest height. A curious crowd followed us through the streets. Jehoiakim must have had warning, for he met us on the palace steps.

"The prisoner," I said heavily.

"Treasonous swine," he leered. "Thought you would stir up trouble in Egypt?"

Uriah raised his head and looked squarely at Jehoiakim. *A proud defiant nabi*, I thought. *I wish there was room for you in our world.* I said, "Your orders, sovereign king of Judah?"

"Kill him," he ordered shrilly.

"By order of the king," I said. Uriah looked my way, but I signaled the soldier whose horse had the tether binding Uriah. The soldier prodded his horse into motion. Uriah moved too, forced to turn from me. I took my short sword out of its sheath. Leaning forward and a little to the right, I drove my sword hard and fast into the small part of his nape. I felt the blade point deflect slightly on his collarbone, then continue, passing through the throat at an angle. I did not stop my downward thrust until my sword hilt rested on his neck. His knees buckled. Blood gushed up over my arm. His body slipped off the blade and he fell forward. The soldier's horse shied and stamped nervously at the fresh-blooded carcass still bound to his saddle. I grunted, "Keep moving all, parade pace." My little regiment rode slowly out of the palace square toward a stable. Uriah's blood trailed after us in a dark line on the pavement stones.

The crowd drifted away. One more nameless criminal had been disposed of. By evening, he would be forgotten.

Something else I learned early in my training: if you have to execute someone, distract him if you can, even for an instant, just before you strike. It is an acceptable act of mercy. Uriah had at least been given that much. He never saw my blade.

In the fourth year of Jehoiakim's reign, Nebuchadnezzar killed three hundred and fifty thousand Assyrians and seventy-five thousand Egyptian troops. Throughout the Fertile Crescent it came to be known as the carnage at Carchemish, the city where the Assyrians made their last frantic stand. Egypt had merely lost a field army hundreds of miles from her borders. It was the end for Assyria. Egypt's chained yard dog was now a stinking carcass, too huge even for an orderly burial. The Carchemish carnage also marked the beginning of a winner-take-all struggle for the western part of the Fertile Crescent. For five years we watched, like a small child might watch his parents fight, crouched in the creases of our land, hoping we would not come to harm through some careless misstep of the two combatants, Egypt and Babylon.

At first we continued sending gifts to mother Egypt. Then we sent them to father Babylon. Jehoiakim chafed at his new master. Nebuchadnezzar did not fuss over him as the Egyptians had. For everyone else, it did not really matter. The love of either parent could not be bought. The best we could hope for was that we would not be abused.

After five years of living in a crouched posture, jumping at every sound, and Jehoiakim could endure it no longer. Patience and forbearance had never been his distinguishing features. Nebuchadnezzar, having pushed Egypt back to her own borders, returned to Babylon in great haste. His father had died, and he could not be crowned emperor in absentia. Besides, who knew what intrigue festered in Babylon? My private opinion was that all kingdoms in the world suffered from the lice of deceit and betrayal.

After a year during which Nebuchadnezzar did not return, Jehoiakim stopped sending tribute. "He will not come back," declared Jehoiakim when the council met to hear this new decision. "Sedition in Babylon will force him to remain where he is. Now is the time for bold action: what my father, Josiah, started, I will complete."

"In this you are mistaken," replied Gemariah, brother to Ahikam. "Nebuchadnezzar will not rest until he has walked the streets of Memphis." I liked this Gemariah, who spoke out boldly in the council. He was a junior secretary, and if he felt the freedom to speak, perhaps

Jehoiakim's hold on power was not absolute. In the end, Jehoiakim's decision was not changed. I marveled sadly at the consequences that come from a son still competing with his dead father. Under Josiah, we had enjoyed liberty. But under Jehoiakim, our national policy was dictated by the ego of a spoiled boy intent on cutting a larger path through the meadow than his father.

Nebuchadnezzar did not come. Instead, we were attacked by well-supplied guerrilla troops from base camps in the Arabian wilderness. They wore no uniforms and never showed themselves in large force. It is the worst kind of warfare, empty of all honour. But it is so effective. They targeted our countryside directly. Victories were counted in burned fields, stolen harvests, raped women and torched villages.

My own jurisdiction to the south of Jerusalem was hit hard and often. You cannot win against guerrillas. The best you can hope for is not to lose too badly. I learned how to sleep on my horse, for we patrolled constantly. When we could anticipate an attack, the fighting was fierce and one-to-one. Always, the marauders would retreat, melt away back into their desert sanctuaries only to surprise us somewhere else. Nebuchadnezzar's gold kept them motivated and well supplied. They fed our stolen grain to their horses and after two seasons I knew we could not sustain ourselves.

Already the more remote villages had been abandoned in favour of ravines and hillside caves. Our cities remained untouched, but weariness settled on the countryside like a burial shroud. I cursed Jehoiakim's independence each time I buried a soldier or slit the throat of another horse gone lame.

News that Nebuchadnezzar had left Babylon with a large army, including siege equipment, triggered a national crisis. The Yahweh priests organized a kind of solemn assembly. They proclaimed a time of fasting and orchestrated long sessions of public prayer in the temple courtyard. The prophets came out in droves and the oratory rose high, if not the prayers. If nothing else, panic was kept shut up. In winter, I was summoned to Jerusalem, presumably for new orders. There were no more harvests that could be burned.

About twenty of us had gathered in the council room, talking informally, when Gemariah burst in. He was clutching a scroll, and I wondered at first if it was a royal communiqué from the Babylonians.

"This scroll was read at the temple at this morning's assembly," he began. "It is the oracles of Jeremiah, one of the more outspoken *nabis* in our city. His scribe, Baruch, read it from a high window." He gestured to the man who had followed him in. "Jeremiah has been banned from the temple area."

"But why bring it to us?" someone asked. "What need have we for entertainment meant for the masses?"

"This one is different," replied Gemariah.

"In what way?" asked Ahikam, his brother.

"I did not hear all of it," blustered Gemariah, "but the people have been seized by a great melancholy."

"Melancholy?" asked a voice.

"A kind of holy dread—fear."

"Perhaps it's time we end the fast—too long without food addles the wits."

"What does the scroll say?"

You would do well to listen to it yourself," answered Gemariah. "I have brought Baruch to read it for us."

Ahikam nodded. Someone brought a chair for Baruch and Gemariah led him to it.

"These are the oracles of Jeremiah, the words of Yahweh he has received since he was first commissioned. Some have already been voiced in public and some have not been made known until today. This—" Baruch lifted the vellum in his hand—"is the finished work. I have been a year making it." Only a hint of his professional pride could be detected.

> For twenty-three years—since the time of Josiah— Yahweh has given me words of warning. Again and again, I have spoken them, but you have not listened.[15] Time and time again you have forsaken me, choosing instead the gods of this land. Was it these gods that brought you out of Egypt? Yet you pant after them and spill your seed in homage at their altars. You fondle their images in your imagination until you are inflamed. They ask nothing of you. How can they, since they are the projections of your own hearts?
>
> So know this, O people of Judah, you who think

the walls of my holy city cannot be breached; know this
you false prophets who promise "peace in our time:"
Nebuchadnezzar is my servant. He marches toward your
city because I have ordered it. He will utterly destroy you.
Jerusalem will become an object of horror and scorn. For
seventy years you will live as one with a ring through his
nose; like a slave you will be exiled to a distant land. For
my wrath will not be quenched and my anger comes to
you from the north.

Baruch's voice droned on in careful, measured tones. The work
had been well edited. It was a careful crafting of plain speech, poetic
metaphors, wild, funereal laments and scathing historical commentary.
It reasoned with us, cajoled us, wept over us and raged against us. The
scroll roared and bellowed in rage at our indifference. It whimpered in
pain—the pain of a rejected lover who had given without reservation.
It roared the pain of a lion with a thorn wedged in its paw. The scroll
reasoned with our petty prejudices, appealed to former days when
fidelity had been sweet, like dark red wine. It promised restoration and
pardon. It crooned a love song. It tantalized us with the possibility of
intimacy unfettered by rituals. Finally, it broke into a terrifying bellow
at the total desolation that awaited us. The whips of pestilence, famine,
war and death would descend on our lewd nakedness that we showed
off brazenly to other deities. We had played the harlot and Yahweh's
patience was exhausted.

But perhaps not. Buried in the cadence that filled the room there
was a muted theme of hope. I heard it clearly. Even at this late stage of
our infidelity, perhaps the worst could be avoided. Baruch read: "Bow
your neck under Nebuchadnezzar's yoke; submit to his rule and you
will live. I will spare my city. But if you resist, the sword, famine and
plague will descend on you all."[16] Here was a small window of escape.

The scroll was majestic in its range of voice. Even to me, who did
not read literature, it went beyond the power of clever rhetoric of merely
trying to be heard among competing oracles. These words were the
words of something greater than the *nabi* who had composed them and
the scribe who had put them into neat columns on ivory vellum. The
whole piece was like burnished gold, rubbed into a deep lustre. These
were not the careless rantings of a cut-rate *nabi* seeking a coin.

Quite apart from the style, the argument the speech posed was a bold one, audacious even. Yahweh had declared our future and, whether we liked it or not, the Babylonians were going to rule us. We were wasting our time in our temple antics, seeking his protection. He'd already decided the outcome. Our only choice in the matter was to walk meekly into the exile or to resist and flirt with total annihilation.

It was a monstrous inversion of the way gods operated. Your own god always protected you. When calamity struck, it was because some other more powerful god had gained ascendancy. But Yahweh was taking responsibility for what awaited us—for what awaited all the nations, for that matter. It was preposterous. Punishment at the hands of your own deity—against his own throne and temple.

But were the oracles reliable?

Removed from the usual context of a crowded market place or temple square, the words hung in the room, suspended by their own authority. I pictured them like small, winged soldiers, set loose from the scroll by their reading, resplendent in their uniforms, parading in solemn formation past our vision. They filled the room—archers, chariots, footmen, horsemen, siege wagons, battalion after battalion—marching in time to the cadence of Baruch's voice.

The room was silent after Baruch had finished. The people had been right to be fearful. So, I think, were we.

So this is how religion works, I thought. But there was no time to think through all that that might mean.

Elishama, the secretary, took the scroll from Baruch's hand and, drawing him to his feet, said, "You are not safe here. Go, together with Jeremiah, and hide yourselves. No," he said, stilling the protest on Baruch's lips, "do not tell us where you will be."

"But my scroll," managed Baruch. He was more anxious for the treasure being wrested from his hands than he was about his safety.

"Leave it with us. Others will have to hear it. We will keep it safe. You have our assurances."

After Baruch left, Elishama set the scroll gingerly on a table. No one seemed inclined to touch it. "So what to do?" asked Ahikam.

"Jehoiakim must be told," I said. "Perhaps it will move him from the present plan of holding out against Nebuchadnezzar."

"Who will tell him?" asked Elishama. There was a long silence and I could feel the room turn to me.

Finally Gemariah said, not unkindly, "You are, after all, his father-in-law."

Elishama put the scroll in his room. I went in search of my son-in-law. I found him in the south wing of the palace—we called it the winter quarters, since it retained heat a little better than some of the other sections. A large shallow brazier burned in the centre. He'd been in the room for some time, judging by the smoke and the mess of cups and plates scattered on a table close to him. The fast seemingly had not applied to him.

"Elnathan, come, enter. A drink to chase away this cursed cold? No?" He seemed put out that I would decline. "What news have you brought?" he asked, looking at my face.

"There has been a public reading of certain oracles, Jehoiakim." I picked my words carefully, as if I were sorting glass shards. "They are commanding—arresting—in their brilliance."

"Oracles? From a diviner? Are there any left in our city?"

"Oracles from a prophet of Yahweh," I replied.

"Do we know him?" Jehoiakim's brow knit.

"Jeremiah is their author, although someone else read them."

"Jeremiah, the one who caused us trouble before?"

"The same," I replied.

"And so what of them?" he asked.

"They have stirred the people, made them uneasy in fact. Several of the council thought it prudent to hear them for ourselves—to know their content directly. We have just finished hearing them."

"And?" pressed Jehoiakim.

"And you should hear them too," I blurted, but I spoke the words too quickly and cursed myself for the implied fright. I felt revulsion for having stooped to persuade this rake to hear literature of which he was not worthy. "You will not like them. They speak against your belief that Nebuchadnezzar can be withstood. In short, they will make you furious. But . . .", I broke off.

"But what?"

"The council feels you should hear them," I finished stiffly.

41

"Then hear them I shall," said Jehoiakim. "There," he smiled, patting my arm lightly, "that wasn't a difficult message to deliver, was it?"

So for the third time that day the scroll was read. We all crowded into the winter quarters. Our numbers had tripled to about sixty, almost the full roster of our court's administration. A junior scribe, Jehudi, was summoned, and Elishama delivered the scroll to him for reading.

"Begin," said Jehoiakim, once he had settled himself in his chair close to the firepot.

Jehudi began. He read about two columns of words.

"Stop," declared Jehoiakim. Rising, he approached Jehudi's stool. "Give me your scribe's blade." It was a short, very sharp knife, part of every secretary's equipment. It sharpened styli and scraped old inks from parchment. Jehudi produced it. Jehoiakim took one end of the scroll, the part just read. He continued to stand over Jehudi, who held the larger part. Carefully, keeping tension on the scroll, Jehoiakim cut the two columns from the scroll.

I have heard men's dying screams that touched me less than that rasp of slit vellum. But Jehoiakim wasn't through with his entertainment. Swinging round to the brazier, he let the tiny leather strip of words drop onto the coals. It sizzled and the oils from both skin and ink let off a dark, pungent smoke. I thought of incense as I watched it.

"These words are useful. They give us warmth," laughed the king. "Jehudi, please read us more."

Jehudi read. Jehoiakim cut and burned the scroll at intervals. Some watchers, like myself, sat stupefied. Others, taking their cue from the king, laughed and joked along with him.

The scroll was about one third gone when I jumped to my feet. Jehoiakim tossed another strip toward the coals. My hand darted forward and snatched the vellum from his hand. It was mine, although I didn't know what force had moved it.

"Stop this madness, this insolent destruction," I cried. This scroll is not a trifle to be hacked apart in an afternoon's amusement."

"Release the parchment from your hand and put it on the fire," Jehoiakim said icily.

"Jehoiakim, disagree with the words if you must. Mock them, make sport of their author. Be the first among us to refute them with wit. And

42

I, I will laugh if you so order it. But do not cut and burn such literature. It . . . it cuts — at who we are."

"Elnathan, put what is in your hand in the fire."

"O King, all of Judah is in the city seeking assurances that we will not be laid waste by Nebuchadnezzar," I continued, "who approaches from the north. Always, in times of crisis, the prophets of Yahweh have been allowed their voice. It is an honoured tradition. In times past, their words have saved us. Did not Micah give good counsel to your forefather, Hezekiah?[17] Did not Isaiah stand before the throne of Ahaz?"

Gemariah, who stood against a far wall, spoke loudly so the whole room could hear. "Jehoiakim, the masses already attach credence to this scroll. You risk further unrest when they learn it has been destroyed."

Jehoiakim appeared not to have heard. He had not once taken his eyes from my face.

"Burn what's in your hand, Elnathan. Your king commands it."

I watched my hand grip the scrap tightly, knuckles white from the tension. No one else spoke. In my peripheral vision, I noticed two of the palace soldiers move ever so slowly closer to me.

"By order of the king," I croaked. I opened up my hand and the twisted bit of leather dropped to the coals. I fled the room, pursued by laughter.

———

I sulked and fumed in Lachish, swore at my men and painfully executed two unfortunate Arab renegades we'd been able to capture. Jeremiah's words marched through my head endlessly. The smell of burning leather ambushed my nostrils. The scent so strong that I would turn, expecting to see a fire somewhere.

Questions crowded me, of a kind I'd had no training in. Who was this jealous God of ours that promised such punishment, yet would not abandon us? We would be cut back, but not cut off. And if the oracles were reliable, Jehoiakim was a fool if he thought he could slip the cords that bound us to this God simply by burning them. Some deeper magic was afoot, I concluded. The gods of Baal, Ishtar and Molech—they did not pursue us if we ignored them for a time. They took us back without consequence. They never sent such articulate missives. Truth was, they never spoke to us at all. But this Yahweh, he hounded us. His religion was an active thing. We could not escape it, even if we could escape the temple. Now it would seemed our destiny was to bend our necks in the service of Nebuchadnezzar. If this were the pleasure of a God whose jurisdiction had no boundaries, what impudence had seized our king to defy the will of our God?

But was the scroll true?

If it was, then I'd killed a loyal man in Uriah, and Jehoiakim's defiance was the ultimate treachery. What would Yahweh do to me for having executed his servant? I sensed some individual decision being thrust at me. I resisted swallowing it, like strange food on my pallet.

———

When news came that Nebuchadnezzar had reached Riblah, sixty miles north of Jerusalem, I made up my mind.

Riding hard to Jerusalem, I found the city preparing for a long siege. The warehouses bulged with grain sacks. Our streets were full of villagers seeking protection.

"What does the council say?" I asked my father.

"The council has not been formally convened for some time," he replied.

"Have we sent emissaries to seek an accommodation?"

"None have gone."

"Do we know the strength of his force?"

"He is en route to fight Egypt. We happen to be in his path and he will not leave a pocket of revolt to his backside as he advances. We would become a base of harassment and encouragement to other cities. Each city he has to capture slows him down and diminishes his field strength."

"Can we expect Egyptian reinforcements?"

"They offer prayers on our behalf, daily, from the safety of Memphis."

"What is the condition of our city?"

"Our food supplies will carry us perhaps two years. The water tunnel is in good repair."

"But?"

"But the Babylonians have brought Persian sappers, an expert corps of engineers. They are the ones who brought down the walls of Ninevah. Still, we have held off large armies before. The city of Tyre is in its third year of siege and its walls have not been breached."

"A different tactical situation entirely," I replied. "They are a seaport, built almost entirely on an island. What idiot tries to gather hope from them?" My father did not answer.

"Jehoiakim's mood?" I asked finally.

"Brazen, when with wine. Ashen when not."

I ate that night with Acbor. Afterward I excused myself and walked quietly to the palace. No one challenged me. It was the privilege of family. Nehushta had retired to her chambers and her maid showed me in.

"Father!" She looked awful. I did not know what to say to her. I drew close and hugged her awkwardly.

"Where is your husband?" I asked finally. "I have news."

"On the rooftop."

"I will try to come back to you, perhaps tomorrow. I've just arrived in the city." A door from her chambers led out into a private passage from where I could access the upper levels. I started toward the roof.

"Elnathan!" Jehoiakim seemed genuinely glad to see me. He was alone. The palace was built tight against the northern city wall. Closest to the wall Jehoiakim had built a small garden—a pretty little enclosure. He sat on a cornice, sideways, that had been notched into the city wall about three feet below its top edge. He gazed northward, toward Riblah.

"I've come to make amends," I said, sitting down. "I was foolish . . . and showed no respect."

"Your king forgives you," he said in mock formality.

"I can be certain of your pardon?" I asked, responding in the same tone.

"Come, feel the warmth of my embrace." He laughed, getting up. The relief he felt at my apology was evident; he'd missed me. Strange indeed.

I put both my hands on his back, as he did on mine, beginning the traditional hug that men will give each other. My left hand moved smoothly to where his neck began and in the same movement I drew my other hand away as if to end the embrace. It moved back, off his shoulder and quickly to his chin. I pushed hard upward, against my left hand, which served as pivot. His neck cracked hard and clean. I tilted him away from me and he disappeared, head first, over the city wall.

Epilogue

Following Jehoiakim's death, his son, Jehoiachin, was made king. When Nebuchadnezzar finally did march on Jerusalem, the city gates were opened to him without protest. Jehoiachin was taken captive, but only ceremonially bound in chains and taken to Babylon. He lived there as a royal hostage for the rest of his life. The queen mother, Nehushta, Elnathan's daughter, was taken with him. Altogether, 3,023 Jewish nobility, artisans, military officers and merchants were taken into exile (Jer. 52:28). A substantial amount of the temple treasury was also taken at that time.

Historians are generally agreed that Jehoiakim was murdered. By comparing several sources, the consensus is that Jehoiachin was crowned on December 8, 598 BC. His prompt surrendering of the city to Nebuchadnezzar points to a coup. His father, Jehoiakim, would have been thirty-six years old, unlikely to have died from natural causes. Two oracles proclaimed by Jeremiah (Jer. 36:30 and 22:19) promised Jehoiakim's violent death and humiliating burial. It would have made good tactics to leave the rotting body of the former king as a trophy to be given to Nebuchadnezzar.

Since Jehoiachin was taken as a hostage to Babylon, Nebuchadnezzar appointed a new viceroy. Zedekiah, Josiah's third and youngest son, was established on the throne. He would be Jerusalem's last king.

Endnotes

[1] The story of Uriah's execution may be found in the Old Testament book called Jeremiah, chapter 26 at the 20th verse. Fragments of certain military letters (*ostraca*) were found at Lachish in 1935. One military officer named Hoshaiah, who patrolled the land between Lachish and Jerusalem, wrote to his superior at Lachish and complained of a certain prophet (*nabi*) who "weakened the hands" of the troops. While the serious effect that prophecies of defeat and captivity had on the morale of troops is substantiated, the actual name of the prophet remains conjecture. Some scholars have attributed this reference to Uriah but it is inconclusive.

[2] Elnathan is mentioned only twice: once in Jeremiah 26:22 and the second time in chapter 36:25. His father did serve at the court of Josiah and must have been a Yahweh follower since he was sent to visit Huldah, a prophetess, on behalf of the king. Though we do not know that Elnathan was a military officer, it is plausible to think he might have been in light of his assignment to go to Egypt and capture Uriah. Since he is also mentioned in one of the letter fragments found at Lachish, I have made this his home town.

[3] This person was a senior military commander stationed at Lachish.

[4] II Chronicles 34:14ff; also in II Kings 22ff; Acbor, Elnathan's father, was one of three men sent to enquire of a prophetess whether God was going to punish the people for having abandoned the prescribed liturgies of Yahweh worship for so long a time.

[5] II Kings 22:20; the murder of the pagan priests in the northern territory is specific. See also II Chronicles 34:5. The less precise phrase "did away with" is used of the Jerusalem priests.

[6] II Chronicles 35:8 lists Conaniah, Shemaiah, Nathaniel and his brothers, and Hashanah as contributors to the Passover feast.

[7] Jeremiah 7 and 15

[8] Israel's prophets were conflicted in their attitude toward Assyria. They recognized Assyria as being the agent of God's necessary punishment on Israel. At the same time, they announced Yahweh's eventual annihilation of Assyria in judgment for its barbaric atrocities. See: Isaiah 10:5ff, 14:24ff, Zephaniah 2:13ff, Nahum chapters 1-3, Habbakkuk 1: 5-11. Frequently Babylon is specifically cited as the agent for Assyria's destruction.

[9] Jeremiah 22:10ff

[10] Portions of this speech are taken from Jeremiah 22:13ff. Although it is Jeremiah who says the words, we are told that Uriah said "similar things."

[11] A direct comparison to these two cities, whose sexual practices led to the English word "sodomy," can be found in Jeremiah 23:22. The story of these two cities' punishment is in Genesis, chapter 19.

[12] Jeremiah 13:27, also elsewhere

[13] Ahikam is mentioned in Jeremiah 26:24 as having defended Jeremiah against the charge of treason.

[14] Jeremiah 22:16ff

[15] Jeremiah 25:3ff. The text is a loose paraphrase of several oracles recorded in the book of Jeremiah. The canonical account of Baruch's reading and the subsequent events starts in Jeremiah, chapter 36.

[16] Jeremiah 27:12ff. This particular promise was actually made to Zedekiah, Israel's last king, whose political circumstances paralleled Jehoiakim's.

[17] A reference to the prophet Micah (700 BC) and Hezekiah, then king of Judah, is located in Jeremiah 26:17. It was used there as part of an argument for sparing the life of Jeremiah who was on trial. Micah's oracles are in a book bearing his name. The canonical story of Hezekiah's reign can be found in II Kings, chapters 18-20. It is also in II Chronicles, chapters 29-32. It is noteworthy that the prophet Isaiah foretold the capture of Jerusalem, and the exile in Babylon to Hezekiah, (II Kings 20:6ff). At the time the warning was given, Babylon was still a city-state within the greater Assyrian Empire.

SHAHEENA

I t was not until her third pair of sandals gave out that Shaheena[1] realized just how very far from home she was. She had put off the decision about her sandals until the morning, preferring to examine them in the sharp natural light rather than the uncertain flickers of the evening cooking fire. Sure enough. As she suspected, a hole the size of her index finger had formed in the sole at ball of her foot. She pushed her finger through the sole. It was a small, unconscious gesture, yet she began to cry.

Ezekiel, her husband, found her hunched on a small rock, not moving. Around her was all the noise and ordered chaos of a large caravan breaking camp to begin another day's march.

"It's time," he said. She stood slowly and it was then he noticed her tears.

"I'll need new sandals from the cart," she answered, offering the one that now dangled from her extended finger. "I have only one pair left."

She watched his slight, wiry frame dart off toward the baggage cart. He returned with the same sense of energy, his eyes anxiously assessing her mood.

"I'll find new ones for you at Babylon," he said.

"My husband, the shoemaker priest." She forced a smile. The moment had passed safely. She would continue.

Babylon. For three months now they had trudged toward that word. Three thousand of Jerusalem's more talented citizens, together with their Babylonian escorts. There were not many old people among them. Few had ever been more than fifty miles north of their birthplace. Shaheena was only seventeen and Ezekiel barely twenty, married

53

for all of four months. *Bab-ee-lon*. She could not even pronounce it consistently, so strange did it sit on her tongue. It was a sound that changed each day with her moods, this amorphous destination that drew them from over the horizon.

Jerusalem. For three months now they had marched steadily away from all that was familiar to her. The details of leaving had diverted her emotions from the full significance of the journey. It had all been abrupt and rushed. Here on the road, despite the relentless sun that grew hotter each day, she felt as if she had entered a deep cloud. Neither what she had left, nor what she was walking toward was in sight. And like fog that obliterates the landmarks, all too quickly the trek had become a tedious repetition of the same day: the same cold food, eaten hurriedly in the morning; the routine of collapsing their tents, gathering the blankets and kits, stowing them in the baggage carts; then marching another dusty thirty miles. Even the order in which they marched was the same, like a swarm of bees flying in formation, so that all she really saw with any clarity was the backs of those who walked just ahead of her.

Ezekiel was comfort. He at least remained sharply delineated. She wondered, though, to what extent his confidence was for her benefit. His intense care was mixed with traces of guilt.

The road to Babylon had gone first north, up as far as Carchemish, a city where the Babylonians had successfully beaten down the Assyrians. Shaheena knew this had been a decisive moment in the world events of her age. It was the end of the Assyrian Empire and its grip on the Fertile Crescent which had lasted two hundred years. She was not stupid or dismissive of world events. But at the level she lived—the level of each tedious day of the march—there was nothing to give significance to the fierce conflict that had occurred. It meant only that the military dress of her guards was decorated differently, and that the guttural cacophony she listened to was of a different pitch and cadence. It meant only that they were marching to Babylon instead of Nineveh. But both these cities were just words.

She knew—in the singsong way a child knows and recites things by rote—why she happened to be marching. Not content with victory at Carchemish, the Babylonians, under their leader, Nebuchadnezzar, had continued south, intent on doing battle with Egypt. Jerusalem was simply on the way. Were it not for the reckless impudence of the Jewish king, the city would have purchased its peace with the usual tribute and genuflection. But Jehoiakim, their young king, had not paid tribute to the new overlords, betting that Jerusalem could withstand a siege longer than Nebuchadnezzar could deploy his army in the field so far from his homelands.

Jehoiakim had died. His body was found in a crumpled heap outside the city wall. The official conclusion was that he had fallen from his rooftop garden. He was probably pushed. For the city, it was a convenient death. His son, Jehoiachin, had opened Jerusalem's gates with civility, grace and much haste. Nebuchadnezzar, pleased with this display of common sense, had not destroyed Jerusalem or killed Jehoiachin. Instead, he sent the entire royal family to Babylon, along with about half the treasury. He had also demanded three thousand hostages—the young and talented elite, who would be the most obvious instigators of any future rebellion. Shaheena was part of an insurance policy. That was why she was marching.

But what she knew—knew in her heart—was the guilty anguish that had seized the city's families while the three thousand were chosen. It felt like child sacrifice on a grand scale. She remembered Ezekiel bursting into their small apartment, words spilling out of his mouth with the news that he had been allowed to go as one of the temple priests. He was a caged cat that night, pacing round and round their table that stood in the centre of their room.

"Allowed?" she had finally asked. "You asked to go?"

"I feel it is my destiny," he had answered, held in some magic power wrought by his own words. "Yahweh's hand is in this, of that I am sure, although the details remain a mystery."

"Ezekiel, all over the city people are looking for ways to avoid going. I know of two fathers who have hidden their sons, and you have committed us to go—without speaking first to me?"

They stood with the table between them, the unsteady light of the oil lamp playing across their faces. *So this is what marriage brings*, she thought. *He decides for both of us.*

He did not answer her, yet neither did he avert his eyes. She watched his face as he silently petitioned her to understand the intensity with which he desired to go—aware of her shock, and yes, perhaps his betrayal, yet not willing to revisit the decision.

In the time it takes to blow out this lamp, she thought, *you have severed me from everything familiar. Yet your face asks that I accept.*

"For how long will we be gone?" she asked finally. Ezekiel adjusted his wide linen belt. "I do not know."

But there is something that you do know and are not telling me. The decision to go lay between them, as solid an obstacle as the table.

By the time she visited her father, Baruch, that evening, he had already heard the news. Shaheena's parents were estranged and she had grown up in the household of Baruch's parents. She loved her father, and Baruch, having deprived her of a mother, cared for her with the passion of two parents.

She found him at his writing stool. He was a scribe by profession. He ran toward her and they clung fiercely to each other, awkwardly, tightly, neither able to initiate closure.

I may never hold him again, she thought. She pushed her face harder into his shoulder, smelling his scent and memorizing the feel of his robe as it surrounded her face.

I will never see her again. It was Baruch who finally pushed her back so that he could look at her, but he did not let go. Shaheena's long black hair hung clear of her round face and her eyebrows, pronounced and circular, arched high. Baruch spoke. "I have already collected writing supplies for you. There will be couriers to take our letters. It is fortunate that you can write for yourself." He paused, then hurried on. "Your grandmother is already assembling food and household provisions. She packs as if you were heading into the wilderness instead of to the biggest city on earth."

"Why do I have to go?" she asked.

"You've been chosen," he replied.

"Ezekiel volunteered. He pressed to go."

"That is a good way to approach this adventure, with eagerness."

"This city, you, all of this—it is my home."

Baruch laughed. "I wonder if Abraham's wife said the same thing when she left to come here."

"Did Abraham come from Babylon then?" she asked, confused by his remark.

"From not far away. It was a city called Ur, in the same region. You are going to an ancient place, a city some say goes back even to the time of Babel.

"Could you not come with us, Father?"

"My place is here, just as yours is with Ezekiel and the others. He is your husband. He needs you." Baruch spoke the words without force, almost casually. They were the hardest words he had ever uttered.

That was the nub of it. She would follow the man she had married—this thin, short man, whose ribs she could feel with her fingers when they lay together, whose impertinent opinions about the temple rituals were already getting him into trouble with his superiors; this man who, once having settled his mind on a thing, could never be dissuaded—this was the man she would follow. This was the Ezekiel who would not apologize for what he had done. And it was an Ezekiel who did not need her in the least.

But she would follow the other Ezekiel—the Ezekiel who, in the early hours of the morning, would lie restlessly beside her, twitching as if to shake off a fly. It was this Ezekiel that she would pull toward her, curling her body so that her breasts pressed tightly against his taut back and her arm covered his chest. She would bury her face in his neck, willing her hot breath to banish his nocturnal visitors. Baruch was right. There was an Ezekiel who needed her very much and, what was more, to embrace his destiny as well.

Later that night, in the darkness of their apartment, she reached out to him. Afterward he stayed on top of her and she could feel a warm wet sheen that started between her legs and spread upward onto her stomach and small, hard breasts—a mixture of semen and sweat. In the comforting fog that heralds sleep, she pictured Abraham and Sarah clinging to each other somewhere in a place called Ur, the seed of Abraham cementing their two lives. Ezekiel's slight body lay still and warm.

———

Ezekiel had always dreamed, but not in a way he thought unusual. He was a priest, not a prophet, most of whom he dismissed as cheap entertainers pretending to be divine emissaries, augurs who sold

Yahweh's opinions to just about any inquirer. Yahweh's usual form of communication to them was through dreams, or at least that is how they said it was done. For a larger fee, visions could be summoned, and for the super rich, a special omen could be arranged. Yahweh, it would seem, prattled endlessly about a glorious future that lay just past the current difficulties. Prophet and patron alike ignored the grubby truth that good news always fetched more money than bad news. The real commodity being sold was peace of mind. The more chaotic the affairs of state, the brisker the business.

Not that Ezekiel thought the priests were a whole lot better. Despite the reforms attempted by a former king, Josiah, the priests' guild was equally commercial in the exercise of its franchise. The guild competed fiercely for the hearts, and subsequently alms, of Jerusalem's citizens. While Yahweh, whose temple staff enjoyed a royal stipend, was nominally the national patron of Israel, almost everyone kept relations with at least one other heavenly deity. Baal, Ishtar and even Chemosh could all be placated with a grain offering without leaving the city walls. Dual loyalties prevailed everywhere. It was an era of prudence.

It was when he received a dream while he was fully awake that Ezekiel cautiously sought the advice of one of the few prophets he trusted. He had been on duty in the antechamber of the temple. It was a kind of inner sanctuary that housed the incense altar, Solomon's ten large candlesticks and assorted other relics. Along one side stood a low table, sheathed in beaten gold, on which lay ten loaves of showbread. They were replaced daily with fresh ones. Cleaning this room was a duty he loved. He would move about silently, filling lamps with fresh oil, trimming wicks, lighting new incense blocks and carefully brushing up the ashes of the old.

The dream started as he approached the showbread. He was perhaps an arm's length away, reaching to remove the first of the ten loaves, when it moved. The bread had been replaced with some large insect—a grotesquely inflated beetle with two claws extended toward him. The whole table was then alive with large black creatures. They moved quickly. Several dropped off the table and scurried toward the double doors leading to the most holy inner sanctuary, in which stood the ark of covenant. Three of the creatures stayed on the table, clambering over each other, snapping their oversized claws and waving long leathery feelers angrily in the air. Ezekiel must have shouted, although how long he had stood in front of the creatures he didn't know. Another priest was at his side, asking in a loud voice if he was ill. When he looked again, the ten loaves of showbread were on the table just as they had been.

He sought out Jeremiah. Everyone knew that crusty nay sayer who never lost an opportunity to remind Jerusalem of its debauched disregard of Yahweh. In private, he was quiet, gentle and civil. In public, he was a caustic goad which had provoked his arrest on two occasions for inciting a public disturbance and fomenting turmoil. However, on one point, the whole city agreed: Jeremiah's opinions could not be purchased. And because of it, Ezekiel sought him out.

"What was the other vision?" asked Jeremiah when Ezekiel had finished his story. "You said the beetles were the second one."

Ezekiel's face became a study of indecision. Finally he blurted, "I saw the temple on fire. I was climbing the steps just in front of the two main pillars—the broad ones that make up the main entrance. It wasn't even a duty day for me. I was just taking a shortcut back to my chambers."

"And?" probed Jeremiah.

"And suddenly, everywhere I looked were flames—at the base of the main doors, at the pillars, along the porch columns, even on the stone steps themselves."

"I even felt the heat," he added. "But just as quickly, everything was as it should have been. It was so sudden, both in coming into my vision and in leaving, I almost dismissed it as a trick of the sun."

"But you did not."

"No."

"Why?"

"My clothes smelled of smoke afterwards. It was the smell of burnt flesh, from when we slaughter an animal and burn the fatty sections on the altar. Except that there was no fire burning that day, and my clothes were not the ones I wear on duty."

The conversation stopped. Finally Ezekiel asked, " What do these things mean?"

"That is not the question you have come with," answered Jeremiah. More silence hung between them. Jeremiah, twice Ezekiel's age, watched as this outspoken, energetic priest wrestled to find words. Finally, in a voice Jeremiah had to strain to hear, Ezekiel asked, "These things I have seen—are they true?"

"Yes," said Jeremiah. "I believe you are seeing a future."

"Can they be escaped—changed?"

"Perhaps, but I for one do not believe it is possible. Some do. I am not always right."

"But for Yahweh's temple—even the most holy of places—to be defiled, or worse, destroyed, is an assault on his very person. The temple is his home."

"Not if he has left," said Jeremiah.

It was an idea that challenged everything Ezekiel believed and had been taught. Without a temple, Yahweh, Master of the Universe, was inaccessible. But he could not think about this just now—there was another question he wanted answered.

"Jeremiah," he began, "the whole city recognizes you as a *nabi*, a prophet to whom Yahweh has shown himself."

Jeremiah chuckled. "Yes, and frequently tries to kill me in appreciation."

"But was it something you wanted to become?"

"Not at all," he replied. "What person in his right mind would practise a vocation to his own detriment? Who seeks to be perpetually rejected?"

"So why not just stop?"

"I have tried, but in the end I cannot keep quiet. It is like watching a small child wander ever closer to the edge of a cliff. You just can't stand by and say nothing. It is the curse of being chosen."

"Chosen?"

"Chosen, gifted, called, being prescient. Choose whatever fancy label you want. I think of it as being ambushed more than anything else. One minute you're quietly making your way through life, doing the best you can to fit in, and the next minute you find you've been shut out from the world –you've become an observer. You get up in the morning and it's as if your eyes have been fastened over with crystals. No matter how hard you squint, everything is distorted. But not distorted, more as if the things that are on the inside of people can be seen on their outsides. You hear and see everything at two levels. It's like living within a perpetual metaphor, and as much as I try, I cannot find a way out of it."

Jeremiah paused. Ezekiel's face was frozen in bewildered apprehension. He softened his tone.

"Look, Ezekiel," he said, "I stand in the temple square and listen to Hananiah the prophet holding forth to a group of novice priests. He is by far the most persuasive of all the rotund repositories of optimism. His voice is pleasant. He makes small jokes. He speaks to the timid man inside each of us. Moreover, he promises peace and prosperity in the name of our god. Nebuchadnezzar's armies will remain distant news. I see the comfort he bestows and the honour he receives in return.

"But what I also see is a pimp who prostitutes the words of Yahweh, tarting them up into the fantasy of the week. Would that I could consume his soothing pap with the innocence of those who stand around me. Instead, what I eat is great loneliness and it devours my innards." He suddenly put his face quite close to Ezekiel's.

"Don't go looking for visions, Ezekiel. Stay a priest. Do your duty. Marry. Have children. Be content in each day. That is my answer to your question that you did not ask."

In the months before Ezekiel left for Babylon, he did just that. He married Shaheena, the one with the round dark eyes that saw through his outlandish bravado and loved him all the more for it. There were no other visions to disturb him. However, when the chance came to leave Jerusalem, he took it. There was Shaheena to think about now.

―――

The travelers made it to Babylon before Shaheena's last pair of sandals wore through. A month before the city's walls could be seen, the road had leveled and afforded an easy progress through the Euphrates' lush delta lowlands. Villages and hamlets abounded like clusters of grapes on a vine. Where the road ran close to the river she could see boats and barges being pulled upstream by oxen or sculled lazily downstream toward the Persian Gulf. It was a scene of perpetual harvest, parturient with excess. By comparison, her own land of Palestine seemed arid, almost sterile.

She was not, however, prepared for the heat. That last month of travel they had adopted the habit of stopping between noon and three o'clock. The weaker ones would crawl beneath the wagons in a futile attempt to find relief. Sometimes, in the monotony of walking, she would imagine they were being pulled toward some giant furnace, sucked inward like so much fuel. Their escorts were inured, or perhaps it was the military training that stopped them from showing any outer signs of discomfort. The woollen tunics and cloaks that had been welcome in the mountains of Lebanon had long since been replaced with the lightest of cotton shifts. Women did not bind themselves. Modesty became a casualty in the quest for comfort. The more petulant of the exiles complained incessantly, although to whom exactly was never clear. They carried themselves with an injured air, as if the solid sheets of sun were a special punishment the Babylonians had created just for them. For Shaheena, and others who strove to adapt, the whining voices of complaint were like so many whirring gnats that you dealt with best by ignoring them.

They would all remember the day Babylon stood up on the horizon. *Babylon.* The word toward which they had shuffled all these months. Finally, the amorphous image that was part dream, part nightmare, was revealed. Reality replaced imagination and, in so doing, revealed how naïve and sheltered they had been. Nothing could have prepared them for the scale and grandeur of Babylon, for there was no other city like it in existence. Whereas Jerusalem's walls could protect, at most, twenty-five thousand people, Babylon was the permanent home to two hundred thousand. Her citizens came and went through any of seventeen broad gates, whereas Jerusalem had five small openings. A regiment of charioteers and mounted guards kept watch, patrolling steadily over a seventeen-mile brick roadway that defined the top of the walls. Jerusalem's wall could be walked in an hour.

Babylon—gateway to the gods, home to twenty major temples and seven hundred shrines, home to the ziggurat, a seven-story monument where the great god Marduk, Babylon's patron, was said to have first come to earth.

Jerusalem—home to Yahweh, the god who was so invisible that he had only reluctantly permitted the building of one small temple, one hundred feet by thirty feet, not counting the apartments on its perimeter. Even that one temple was shared now by other deities, whose images commanded its rooftop so that it resembled a gaudy bazaar wagon rather than the temple of the one, supreme God.

They were marshaled, that final day of the march, two miles from the western approach in preparation for what was meant to be a formal oblation to their new masters. The Ishtar gate, which they approached to the steady beat of military drums, was specially designed to reduce even the most elaborate display of dignity to a shabby rag-tag march of the dispossessed. The last half-mile of the approach lay between two tall walls that protruded at right angles to the gates proper. Both sides were inset with glazed bricks. Lions, three times actual size, panted just above Shaheena's head. They shared space reluctantly with equally large mosaics of angry bulls, the icon of Marduk. Their gold-glazed flanks radiated against a deep blue background. With each measured step, Shaheena slunk lower, the last dregs of identity lapped up by the tongues of Nebuchadnezzar's welcoming pride. She knew how her group must have looked. She herself had not bathed in days. Her usually shining hair hung dirty, clumping to her forehead in sweat. Her tunic was torn at the hem and her lower legs were criss-crossed with dried rivulets of dirt.

They did not actually enter the city. Shaheena was relieved that she would escape the disdainful examination of the people who lived within. Instead, just at the entrance, a handful of officials mounted a dais and one of them spoke. She was surprised at his fluency in Hebrew.

"It pleases Nebuchadnezzar that you will give of your skills to the furtherance of his city. A camp has been provided for you on the edge of the Chebar River. Practise your crafts, increase the glory of our city and it will go well with you. Oppose the wishes of our king and you will be slaughtered." The man stopped speaking, nodded to the officer in charge of their escort, and the caravan retreated along the gauntlet of lions and bulls they had just traversed. Babylon had swallowed yet one more morsel of conquered humanity.

Their quarters at the Chebar River were a ghetto of one-storey huts clustered at the edge of an irrigation canal that diverted part of the Euphrates. The banks were littered with piles of rubbish from other exiled groups similarly interned. "At least we won't have to walk," Ezekiel said softly.

"Not until we return home," she replied, looking around her.

He did not answer.

———

Life began again. Families moved into huts, whose walls were made of thick, loose stones and baled straw plastered with clay and limestone as a barrier against the sun. Cooking was done outdoors in small open-faced ovens. The more adventurous and ambitious among the group made connections within the city and were accepted for the skills they brought. It was a cosmopolitan city. Chaldeans, Hittites, Phoenicians, Persians, Summerians and even Assyrians mingled easily, comfortable and confident in the strength of Nebuchadnezzar's military dominion. A few of the Jews went to serve Jehoiachin and his family, who had arrived much earlier and in considerably more style. The royal hostages were confined in pleasant captivity within the palace grounds. The trade routes through which the exiles had walked were open to anyone who had the nerve and the capital to invest. Some Jews began to trade. A small cadre of men was even seconded to the Babylonian bureaucracy. In time, some would rise to high levels within the administration.

Around Chebar, the delta soil made for lush gardens and Shaheena found herself in charge of a few acres close to where the Chebar ditch rejoined the Euphrates. She did not go often to the city. Those who did would talk animatedly about the maze of streets and monstrous buildings that quickly stole any sense of direction.

There were some among the exiles who made no effort to graft themselves into the tree of Babylon. Those with enough ready money to buy what they needed pined loudly for the day they could return to Jerusalem. They were strident, pious and eloquent in a way that only idle people can perfect. Shaheena was uncertain how to respond. They were frequent buyers of her surplus produce, clucking their tongues in judgement of her shameful cultivation of this "foreign" soil, predicting with every purchase that "some day you will leave all this behind and then where will your efforts have gotten you?" Shaheena accepted their comments along with their coins in the same gracious way that merchants suffer irritating customers the world over.

In truth, she was happy, probably far happier than if she had remained in Jerusalem. Ezekiel, free from the cloy of Jerusalem's priestly hierarchy, embodied all that set them apart as a people He presided over the Yahwist rites of prayer and sacrifices and buried the few who died according to the prescribed traditions. Ezekiel taught Torah and he led the daily prayers, always facing Jerusalem. He performed sacrifices and he circumcised the newborn males. He copied out the songs of David and offered comfort on feast days that could not be properly celebrated. But he was careful about encouraging a false hope. "Remember our forefathers in Egypt," he would say. "They waited four hundred years for their freedom."

At night, around a fire in the common square, he would recite their history: stories of Abraham, Isaac and Jacob, Moses, who had freed them from Egyptian slavery eight hundred years earlier. Ezekiel knew the songs of King David and the ballads of how he had carved out their homeland—pushing the Philistines and other tribes back from the lands Yahweh had decreed for them. The throne of David had been established in the city of Jerusalem: Yahweh had promised it would be occupied forever.

In the black night air, watching Ezekiel's face and caressed by his voice, Shaheena knew who she was in a way that would not have been possible in Jerusalem. Afterward, in their hovel, Ezekiel would talk and talk, buoyed up by the evening's events.

"We're more Yahweh's people than we ever were in our own homeland," he would say. "Not even the senior priest, Seraiah, with the full force of the temple to prop him up, could foster such a fervent longing for our God."

"It helps to be so far away from everything sacred, I suppose," said Shaheena. "It's your voice that keeps it all in front of our eyes—our city, our god. Strange that we worship him with more devotion than we ever did at home. It helps me believe he has not forgotten our little handful of lost followers—that we have not been singled out for punishment."

For four years Ezekiel and Shaheena lived blissfully in the midst of a collective hope that their confinement at Babylon would be short. Shaheena became pregnant and the couple named the baby Sarah. Letters and caravan gossip flowed between Jerusalem and their small community. Nebuchadnezzar's campaigns in the west were not as conclusive as was reported within Babylon, or so came the word in private letters from home. True, the Assyrians were gone forever, but now Egyptian regiments had begun to occupy Palestine and challenge Nebuchadnezzar's claim to the territory. The Jerusalem viceroy, Zedekiah, appointed by Nebuchadnezzar, was thought to be in discussion with five other small states.[2] Perhaps a coalition could be forged against a common master. With Egypt now committed against Babylon, perhaps real independence was a possibility. Every scrap of news and rumour was devoured by the exiles several times over.

"They are like cows," observed Ezekiel one evening after a long discussion around the public fire pit. "It doesn't matter that they are discussing the same bits of information they have had before them a month past. They insist on returning to it, chewing it over and over."

"Still, it keeps their spirits up," Shaheena said.

"They pretend to be players in a great conspiracy," he replied, "when in fact they are little more than fat matrons exchanging third-hand gossip around the well."

"What news we get is always delayed," she agreed.

"Late and public! Do you really think it's possible for us to know something in our squalid little compound that Nebuchadnezzar doesn't already?"

"Do you think we will ever see home?" she asked. "You never comment one way or the other." They were getting ready for sleep.

He shrugged. "Not for a minute do I believe we are here by some accident. To be sure, I long to see Jerusalem again, to celebrate a real Passover, to see our families. But I do not miss the politics of the priests with whom I served. From this great distance it seems easier to forget the hypocrisy and deceit. The whole guild was corrupt. We didn't really serve Yahweh. He was our meal ticket, plain and simple. Belief wasn't a prerequisite. But out here, it's all we've got."

They lay close together that particular night, touching each other gently. *Strange that I feel so safe when home is so far away,* Shaheena thought as she fell asleep.

It did not last. Every new flotsam of evidence that drifted into the compound fanned the hopes for a quick return to Jerusalem. Inevitably, matters escalated, drawing everyone in, even Ezekiel.

The summons to the city came at first light and was delivered in a loud voice from a mounted soldier wearing the chevron of the palace regiment. He spoke through an interpreter—an effeminate-looking civilian who perched on his horse like a restless bird with a voice that chirped.

"By order of our king—he requires all Jews to assemble at noon today in the receiving square of the palace."

The officer's strong voice rolled through the huts, bringing everyone out. He stopped after each sentence for the interpretation, a bull's bellow interspersed with a chicken's squawk.

"There you will witness the punishment that comes to all who plot treason against our city." There was more detail in his announcement. When he finished, Shemaiah, a member of the ghetto council, asked loudly: "May it please the palace to know how quickly your instructions are put into action. However, may we be enlightened why we, such poor visitors to your city, are involved? There is no treason here."

The guard waited for the translation then spoke again. "Certain trusted servants of the king have sought to supplant him and were discovered in their treason. Among them are –" he fumbled for a scrap of papyrus in his belt—"Telmekiah,[3] son of Maaseiah, and Ahab, son of Kolaiah, both Jews." He shoved the writing away and then added, "Be thankful that Nebuchadnezzar is a gracious king and punishes each man only for his own folly. There were some at the palace who would have made examples of you all. It is enough that you will witness their deaths."

Shaheena and Ezekiel marched into the city, taking turns to carry Sarah. Everyone knew the two men. Both had found good jobs in the commissariat corps of the military. Everyone knew everybody who had come from Jerusalem.

"What have they done?" asked Shaheena. Ezekiel spoke out of the side of his mouth, quietly, as if afraid of being overheard. "They have always hoped for a quick return to Jerusalem. No doubt they were seduced by some intrigue against the throne."

"Traitors?"

"Or martyrs," he replied. "There will be some who will make them into heroes before the day's end."

"And you, Ezekiel?"

"They are arrogant bastards who risked the death of us all. If it was Assyrians we were dealing with, you can be sure all of us would be butchered."

The parade ground was already full when they entered through one of the archways that penetrated the forty-foot walls surrounding the open square. Yet a few thousand more pressed into the square after them. Shaheena hugged Sarah tight against her, ignoring the strain of her four-year-old weight, while Ezekiel did his best to shield them both from the crowd. They were jostled into a good view—at one end of what was in essence a large town plaza, twenty-five men stood tied to tall posts. At their feet lay straw and wood.

"The straw looks wet," muttered Ezekiel. "They've put oil on it." A man standing beside them, also an elder, spoke to Ezekiel.

"Only two Jews out of twenty-five. At least no one can claim this is an entirely Jewish plot."

Shaheena looked around as best she could at the crowd. Other ethnic groups stood together in conspicuous clusters within the general crowd. The sentencing took three minutes. Twenty-five runners then advanced with large torches and tossed them at their appointed stakes. Flames leapt up immediately. The screams followed, and they were followed by the scent of burning flesh and viscera. Shaheena covered Sarah's head with a cloth, making sure she could not see. There was no escape from the smell.

Two hours later they were dismissed. Any news of Nebuchadnezzar's weakness had been grossly exaggerated.

Three days later a courier arrived[4] with more letters from Jerusalem. Ezekiel received one and Shaheena recognized the handwriting on its sealed exterior.

"From Jeremiah," he said when he noticed her watching.

"It's my father's hand and seal," she said excitedly. "Open it."

He slowly broke the clay seal and spread the two end flaps flat so the sheets of papyrus could be unfolded.

"One for you," he said, skimming the salutation of the first sheet, "and two for me," he continued, peering at the remainder. He started to read slowly, in the manner of someone who is both reading aloud and at the same time reading ahead lest some part should be left out.

FROM JEREMIAH, SON OF BUZI AT JERUSALEM, TO EZEKIEL, PRIEST AMONG THE EXILES AT BABYLON: BY THE HAND OF BARUCH, THE SCRIBE.

Greetings and may all be found well with you and your household. Our city remains unmolested, but I fear it is inevitable that our viceroy, Zedekiah, will commit us to some mad act of rebellion. I say this not just as an opinion, but confirmed to me by all that Yahweh has revealed to me. Opinion within the city remains against me. Letters have even been received here from Shemaiah—yes, the leader of your own elders, one and the same person. Beware of his smiling face. His letter condemns me for a raving madman and he insists I be put in chains according to some obscure interpretation of Torah. I survive by the good office of a few friends. Zephaniah is the new chief of the temple and is shielding me from the worst of what some would do to me. He is a true Yahwist, although not able to influence the hearts of those who serve under him.

Ezekiel, would that this letter contained an easier burden, but I saw no other way. The second letter to you is an oracle pressed into my mouth by Yahweh but for the ears of those in exile. It needs public proclamation, and I could think of no one else fearless enough to publish unwelcome news.

Be glad you are a priest and not given to visions. The mind of our God obsesses with the punishment he is storing up for his holy city. Hananiah still spouts, "We are his chosen people. We are his chosen people. His covenants are everlasting." Chosen we are, but for punishment, not

blessings. We have played the harlot once too often. For
this reason, the oracle given me must be made known.
It is your small remnant that Yahweh will spare if you
will bend your necks for a little while. I draw you into
the debate by my request but you know my words are
true, or else I would keep them to myself. Write back and
report on their effect. May Yahweh give you all new ears
to hear.

A BLESSING ON YOU. JEREMIAH.

Ezekiel turned to the last sheet. Shaheena, having laid her own
letter aside, stood behind him, reading along without reticence. The
second letter was not long.

AN ORACLE OF YAHWEH, FOR HIS PEOPLE CARRIED INTO
EXILE FROM JERUSALEM TO BABYLON. FROM JEREMIAH, CON-
FINED IN JERUSALEM, PROPHET OF OUR LIVING GOD WHO SEES
ALL: THUS SAYS YAHWEH:[5]

"Do not be deceived by the dreamers among you.
They promise you release but speak lies in my name.
Instead, build houses and settle. Plant and harvest. Marry
and have children. Give your sons and your daughters
in marriage. Increase in numbers. Do not dwindle away.
Seek the peace and prosperity of Babylon, for therein is
your safety. As it prospers, so also will you. For seventy
years, it shall be your home until I call you back."

And hear also a word from Yahweh about Telmekiah,
son of Maaseiah, and Ahab, son of Kolaiah, who spread
lies among you. Thus says Yahweh:

"I will deliver you into Nebuchadnezzar's furnace
where you will burn before the eyes of all the people. Your
names will become curses."

In addition, for Shemaiah, the elder who seeks to
silence me with slanderous letters, Yahweh has a word
for you:

"Everyone you left in Jerusalem will be extinguished.
Not one of your family will escape the punishments I am
preparing. You will die as one who was an orphan from
birth. So they will bear the stripes for your rebellion

70

against my servant Jeremiah."

Blessings on all who hear these words and receive them. Judgement on those who mock.

BY THE HAND OF BARUCH,

A SCRIBE WHO IS NOT UNKNOWN TO YOU.

Shaheena felt her stomach contract as she took in the letter. "It is not possible. How could he have known? Ezekiel, such predictions—it is the work of a diviner, or worse. And yet my father sits with this man."

"It will give people pause, of that I am certain," Ezekiel said.

"What will you do?"

"Do? I will do what I have been asked to do. A man who is worth ten of me asks that I speak in his name. As it happens, his own words come with their own ... compelling authority." He gave her an enigmatic little grin.

There was a long silence. Shaheena turned to her own letter from Baruch. It was the usual kindly, solicitous inquiry from an anxious father who gave no hint of the chaos that engulfed his own life.

They did not speak much over their meal. Shaheena kept looking at Jeremiah's oracle. It was as if another person was sitting with them. She felt, or imagined she felt, a kind of power extending from it, filling in all the spaces of their hut. Her father had penned it. It was just marks on papyri. Why then did it feel dark somehow?

Ezekiel brooded too. He was not perturbed by Jeremiah's prescience. He knew their history better than Shaheena. Their history was littered with "Jeremiahs" who spoke the future accurately. The timing of this oracle's arrival would go a long way toward giving it credibility. He could picture all the huddled conferences that would spontaneously combust all through their compound after he had read it.

"How could it be?" "How could Jeremiah have known?" "Is the letter genuine?" "Did Ezekiel alter it in some way?" "What does the seventy years mean?" On and on would go the questions. They would probably miss its main point too, dazzled by having just witnessed an oracle come to fruition in all its grotesque detail.

"Shaheena." He looked at her intently. "There will be some, perhaps many, that will shun us after tomorrow. They will want someone to receive their anger—and fear. Since they cannot reach Jeremiah, his herald will be a good substitute."

"What are you trying to tell me?"

"People might make things difficult for us ... for you."

Shaheena laughed, spun round, put her arms around him and after kissing his forehead said, "I am four years ahead on my garden. I have the best seedlings. I know this soil and this heat as few others do. Showing kindness to those who have sat bleating in the wind, noses toward Jerusalem, will be sweet revenge." She laughed again. "Being right lets me overlook all manner of insults. And for them, my prices will increase."

"You are not concerned at all?"

"I am proud. Finally we have heard and the matter is settled. You may know Jeremiah. I know my father. You read what came from his hand. It is enough for me. Just let someone try to malign you. I'll scratch their eyes out."

What did I do to deserve such love? he wondered. He did not trust his voice to speak just then. They stood grasping each other.

But as they were lying together that night, Shaheena said, "I must write my father quickly and tell him to come. Jerusalem, it seems, is doomed."

She has figured it out, thought Ezekiel. *We are the ones who are safe.*

To Shaheena's surprise, the people's response was solemn. The oracle was not rejected out of hand. Some whispered that the entire letter was a fabrication, written locally. The theory did not gain support. Ezekiel's reputation, if anything, was enhanced, as if whatever powers that had first wrought the oracle might extend to its messenger. Ezekiel had been right. It gave one pause. More people became interested in planting gardens, just in case.

———

Shaheena was not worried when Ezekiel did not come home for the mid-day siesta the next day. Even when he did not arrive for dinner she resisted the uneasiness she felt, telling herself he had probably gone to the city and missed the last chance to leave before the gates were shut.

By the morning of the second day, however, she raised the alarm. By midday she knew only that no one had seen Ezekiel. He had simply vanished. For seven days[6] Shaheena and others searched for him. The city was checked as best it could be. Hospices, jails, taverns and even brothels were visited. Bargemen on the Euphrates were asked if they had seen a body.

Two Bedouins brought him back. How they knew where he belonged remained a mystery, as was where they had found him. He was tied to a horse that trotted between the two riders. His head rested to one side of his mount's mane; his arms were pulled forward and tied together around its neck. They wheeled into the open space between the huts and carefully cut Ezekiel down. He lay flat on the ground, staring at the sun. People came running and someone found Shaheena. One of the neighbours' wives brought water. Ezekiel's wide open eyes stared but showed no recognition. His face was badly burned and two broken blisters leaked puss just above his beardline.

He was not dead. Neither was he entirely alive. He seemed to lie suspended between the one space and another, inhabiting two worlds. Sarah went to live with a friend. Shaheena never left Ezekiel alone. He gave no sign that he knew where he was. He accepted drink and broth but the strength gained he wasted in fits of uncontrolled spasms. His hands pawed his face, triggering terrible pain when he connected with his burns. Yet he did not stop. He would thrash from side to side, contorting his body as if trying to escape some external assault.

"His skin must be allowed to heal," a physician warned. "His body fights its own recovery."

Finally Shaheena accepted the obvious and permitted her husband's hands and feet to be tied.

So Ezekiel lay tied[7] to his bed, not speaking, not seeing, a captive now in two realms. Shaheena could get no closer than to dab his sores with salve. When she did, even her most intimate touch went unnoticed.

In time his body healed and the cords were removed. The spasms stopped, although constant twitches took up permanent residence inside him. To a watcher, they seemed like small rodents racing through his limbs. A shoulder would tick, and then a hand would flap. Sometimes an eye would twitch and a moment later a calf muscle jerk. It was as if the aftermath of some great conflict still lingered within. Then came the day when he knew her. It was only his eyes that spoke. No other muscle on his face moved; he made no other gesture. But he had returned to them, and she wept.

> To Baruch, the scribe living at Jerusalem, from Shaheena, among the exiles at Babylon:
>
> Father, greetings and may it be well with you. Sarah grows more quickly than corn. She knows the names of all of her Jerusalem relatives. I have told her all our family stories so often that by now, if I change even the smallest detail, she will correct me. When you come, she will already know you.
>
> It is not well with Ezekiel.

Shaheena put down the pen. *How much do I tell him?* she wondered. *Six months now, and he lives as if under the orders of someone no one can see but him.* She sat in their hut, close to the one lamp she had kept alight. Sarah was asleep. Ezekiel had not slept inside for six months. Instead, he lay in the compound square, on his side. She would check on him before going to bed, as she did every night. By this time it seemed almost normal, as if the square were just another room in their house. She would approach quietly, and if he were awake, they would sit together for a few minutes. She didn't like to leave Sarah for too long.

They did not speak. Ezekiel had not had a regular conversation with anyone since he had come in from the desert. He had tried to speak at first. But his tongue would somehow choke off the words. All he could do was work the back of his throat. A short scale of grunts was now the sum total of his vocabulary with her. She knew from his efforts that not even Ezekiel knew what was happening. He had rasped himself hoarse trying to talk to her those first few weeks. His eyes would grow big and frustrated as he fought for mastery over his tongue. There was much he needed to release, she knew. Eventually he stopped trying. It was better for everyone. Hard to say whose pain was greater: Ezekiel's from trying, or Shaheena's from watching.

She turned back to the letter, keenly aware of her conflicting motives. If she told the truth, in all its bizarre detail, perhaps it might persuade her father to come. If, for some reason, he could not, what was the point of having upset him? As well, there was always the hope that some day, perhaps tomorrow, Ezekiel would recover. Given that the letter would take at least six weeks—maybe several months—to get to Jerusalem, it might all be over by then. Of all the emotions Shaheena bore, it was living always on the knife-edge of hope that exhausted her most. She continued.

> For two hundred days now, he has continued in the same silent pantomime. He started by carving a picture of Jerusalem into a large slab of clay about three feet square. There is no mistaking the city, despite its defects. This he propped up like a wall, supported from behind by a huge mound of dirt. In front, he formed the city's walls from plaster. This construction was easier, and it looks neater than the city scene behind it, whose buildings tilt at odd angles into each other. The wall even has two towers and a gate, and the whole thing is about two feet high. It curves around each end of the "city." I must tell you, father, that in all its crudeness, having our home raised up where we could walk by it all the day lifted everyone's hearts.
>
> His next additions took some time to interpret. Indeed, Ezekiel spent almost two weeks to make them, and still, I notice that he adds innovations covertly. It was a siege army he made, complete with battering ram against the gate, earthen ramps and sappers' trenches. He even shaped small tents.[8] When that was finished, he took a shallow iron griddle, pushed one edge into the dirt and now lies down behind it on his side, staring fixedly at Jerusalem.
>
> The prevailing view is that Ezekiel has been pressed into the service of Yahweh—charged with an oracle so grand, so significant, that he is compelled to act it out for our instruction. Apart from his model building, and his silence, he is in every way as normal as he once was.

Shaheena stopped and read the last part to herself. *I am now telling lies*, she thought. *It is only normal because I cannot bear it if I think of it any other way.* But since she could not erase the thick black liquid that took so long to apply, and was too proud to blot it out, she left it. Normal. She sighed.

There are some things I will decidedly not tell him. I will not tell him that Ezekiel has shaved both his head and face and that he did so in public, with great ceremony. Nor will I tell him that the hair he cut off now sits in three small sacks perched on the city walls. No one has yet found a suitable explanation for what that is supposed to represent.[9]

And I will not tell him that he eats meagrely, cooking on a small fire so that all may see what he does; one small loaf, less than what Sarah eats in the morning, and only half a litre of water. No, I will not tell Baruch that my husband slowly starves himself to death.

She could not endure Ezekiel's slow emaciation. It was all so publicly choreographed. During the morning he would leave his post and scour their village for dried animal dung for fuel.[10] Then in the afternoon, when people would gather, he would carefully measure out exactly eight ounces of meal on a scale he kept just for this purpose. Eight ounces; about a large handful. It baked up into two flat cakes, ten mouthfuls each.

Shaheena had tried to dissuade him, to tempt him with thick soups and roasts. She even took to taking her own meal out to eat with him. Once she sent Sarah with hot date bread, coated in oil, thinking he would not refuse his own child. She came back crying, the bread pressed between her fists.

"He kept shaking his head no," she said. "And he looked angry. I was afraid."

"Your father has received a special message from Yahweh," Shaheena crooned. "It is so important that it must be acted out, like a play we see sometimes in the markets. He is only pretending." She pulled Sarah close. "After the playing is over he will come home. And we will eat and eat until we all fall over into a big heap."

"When, Momma?"

"Soon. Soon, I promise."

She had made one last attempt. Late one night she approached him with slices of lamb, some figs and two oranges she had bought. She had cut them artfully into small chunks. She sat down close to him.

"I cannot let you die, my husband. What good will come of that? Surely that is not the will of the voice who directs you." She reached out and took his hand. He in turn took hers. They stared into each other's faces.

"I am afraid, Ezekiel," she said softly. "This … enactment; must it go on for so long?"

He made to speak but she touched his lips saying, "No, I know that you would tell me if you could. You would tell me all that you have seen, and felt and are feeling now. Would that I could ease your torment."

He simply stared in mute desperation. She continued. "But please, husband, for my sake, at least eat enough to keep your strength. I can bear everything else as long as you don't kill yourself."

They sat, foreheads touching, feeling each other's skin. Leaning forward they hugged and slowly Ezekiel relaxed his head so that it rested on her shoulder. She rocked him gently, stroking the short stubble that passed for hair. She sensed his utter weariness. He began to cry silently into her tunic.

Still he would not eat. And finally she left. Never had she felt such love and such rejection at the same time.

She picked up the stylus to finish the letter.

He is regarded now as both a priest and a prophet. Those who know of such things say that the spirit of Yahweh has not rested on one of us with such power since Samuel lived. Why now, and why here of all places rather than on someone in Jerusalem is the topic of considerable debate. But he is not ridiculed, even for all his antics. He is a kind of holy celebrity among us. The elders treat him with respect—respect and fear. It makes me proud to see that he is taken seriously.

Ezekiel does speak from time to time, Father. Always, though, it is to proclaim an oracle. If he attempts any other communication, his tongue blocks the words so that he has ceased even to try. But there are times when he will begin shouting. He always starts with the phrase, "Thus says Yahweh." He picks his time when there are people around him. I think that is deliberate. Except once when he woke the whole compound up in the middle of the night. We still remember what he said, though!

They are not the rantings of a mad man. His voice

is clear and his thoughts are ordered. He is a commanding orator when these words come to him, quite different
from the Ezekiel who taught us songs and Torah. For me,
Father, the greatest comfort is that when he does speak, he
seeks out every face that will meet his stare. It is in these
brief moments that he connects with us and gets small
respite from his isolation. I can see how much he wishes
to escape his silence. Everyone can.

The meaning of what he is doing is clear. Ezekiel
has even confirmed it in an oracle. I will write here as
best I can recall, because it is not to us that the message
is directed.

Thus says Yahweh: "I myself am against you,
Jerusalem, and I will punish you so that all the nations
will see. Before my anger is exhausted, Jerusalem's elders
will eat their children just to stay alive. They have defiled
my temple and show contempt for my care. So I will
remove myself from you. A third of you will perish from
plague and famine inside your walls. A third will die from
the sword when your walls are overrun, and a third I will
scatter to the winds, only to be pursued."

Father, you are in great danger. Others I am certain
must be sending reports on Ezekiel's oracles since they
have nothing to do with us and everything to do with you.
Inquire elsewhere and you will know that I report faithfully the essential meaning of what my husband says.
Please, I beg of you, come to us and escape before you
cannot. Here there is safety.

BY MY OWN HAND, SHAHEENA

She blew out the lamp. Tomorrow she would find a courier and
send it.

———

"Son of man."

The greeting began faintly from somewhere in the back of his
head. By this time it was familiar. Soon the Euphrates riverbank on

which he sat would fade and he would be led into another reality. The Destroyer was visiting. First would come His four escorts,[11] hideous apparitions with the heads of four animals, three sets of wings and a cluster of whirling wheels that served as feet. Then would come the man—the man whose lower body was a lake of fire and whose upper body was like molten gold.

By this time, the third year of his enforced silence, Ezekiel had learned not to resist. It was futile. There was no predicting when He would come, and Ezekiel had quickly tired from keeping his mental faculties on guard for the assaults.

"Son of man, stand up on your feet, and I will speak to you."

Ezekiel got to his feet. This was always the most stressful part— the beginning, when he was not yet fully swept away. After it started, it didn't matter. Just now, it was like standing in a pit with a large cat hovering at the edge of his peripheral vision. He stood, waiting for the pounce. Knowing he would not die from it was only a partial comfort. Often he had wished he might be killed. That at least would have brought relief.

"Sovereign Yahweh, your servant." He wondered what new thing would be asked of him. The mock siege of Jerusalem had lasted four hundred and thirty days. By the end of it, Shaheena had looked as wasted as he did. Ezekiel's speech was still impeded. Who knew for how much longer?

He had performed other pantomimes since the siege. Once he had traced out a large map of the roads back to Jerusalem.[12] The map was quite large and wandered among a few of the huts closest to the main square. It showed an exaggerated junction at the northern boundaries of Israel. One fork led to Ammonite territory, the other descended toward Jerusalem. Then, each day, he had traced the insignia of Nebuchadnezzar somewhere on the map. It was first placed close to Babylon, then marched ponderously toward the junction. Most everyone made it part of their daily routine to check the location of the insignia, to see where Ezekiel had placed the royal chevron. As it drew closer to the fork, the exiles' tension mounted like a summer cloud building into an inevitable climax. He left the insignia at the junction for a week before moving it in the direction of Jerusalem. There had been no need for an oracle to amplify the meaning of that particular drama.

"You know the things I have prepared for Jerusalem."

"Yes, Sovereign Lord. You have revealed the future to me."

"You know my temple has been defiled?"

"I have seen scorpions infest the holy chamber. You have showed me the elders kneeling on the portico steps[13] but praying eastward to the sun god rather than to you. I have seen your executioners stalk the streets, killing with such speed that I cried out to you to show mercy.[14] Yet your six messengers continued to kill. They killed the young, the old, the virgins and the newly married. Even the infants you did not spare."[15]

"Yet I did not kill them all did I?"

"No, Sovereign Lord. You did not. Some your executioners left to die of starvation and plague. Still others you showed escaping through the broken walls of Jerusalem only to be butchered by Babylonian soldiers who had laid siege. Still others I saw you kept so that they might be burned in their houses as the city was torched. No, Sovereign Lord, your executioners did not kill them all."

"You do not approve?"

"The Sovereign Lord is angry. This much you have revealed to me. And I have been faithful in proclaiming this fact." Ezekiel could not explain, even to himself, how he actually spoke to the person with the fiery gold torso. It felt as if his lips moved, and he heard two voices in his ears. They were the only spontaneous conversations available to him through these years and he approached them with great energy. He had stopped being afraid. The Destroyer was angry? So was Ezekiel. He had not asked to be an ambassador of doom. He had not asked to have his family life ruined. The golden man pressed again.

"But you feel it is unwarranted?"

"You have removed your presence from the temple. Is that not enough punishment for a people that no longer are deserving?"

"Son of man, you are right. My cloud did leave the temple. But tell me, how did the people respond to such punishment?"

Ezekiel knew he was bested. "They did not even know you had left," he answered flatly.

"Eyes they have, but they see not. Son of man, come with me."[16] The body of liquid gold spoke in steady, measured tones, a voice of reason and calm. Ezekiel had learned to trust it. It was what led him safely through the labyrinth back to sanity.

Ezekiel now stood on a narrow footpath somewhere in the hills of Palestine. There were no buildings, only the steep sides of the short stubby mountains that made up most of Israel's countryside.

At the edge of the road lay a baby.[17] She could not have been more than a few hours old. The umbilical cord was ripped, not cut, and hung in a coil beside her. Strands of vernix clung to her like cobwebs. She was howling, but not the usual shrieks of a newborn recently thrust into the universe. They were the shrieks of a thing left to die.

The golden man stooped and picked her up. Ezekiel watched the bloodied skin make contact with the liquid gold of the Destroyer's body. It was a bath to her, and while Ezekiel watched, the baby grew clean. Her body shone with oils. A linen wrap took shape around her. From the face that nuzzled into the Destroyer's chest, turned away so that Ezekiel could not see it, he heard the sound of suck. The golden man crooned into the wrapped bundle. A life had been saved.

The Destroyer placed the baby on the road again. But this time it was no longer a baby but a young girl. She was just on the cusp of womanhood. Breasts stared out at him like small walnuts and her pubic hair was the stuff of velvet gossamer. Hair from her head hung long and straight so that every feature of her face was offered up for frank examination. She wore nothing, yet afterward Ezekiel would say that against her purity, the hills in which they stood looked stained and haggard.

She did not speak, at least not in words. Yet into Ezekiel's head flooded all the speech of adolescence. He heard the wonderment of first discoveries, the exhilaration of accomplishment. He listened to her voice as it moved from the tentative whispers of the ingénue to the dulcet tones of the mature.

When he looked again, before him stood a woman. It was as if the purity of the man's golden fire had entered her, ever so gently sculpting her features so that each tiny detail was a thing of complete perfection. Her hair, still long, lay fuller now with a trace of curl. She held her head high. It was the posture of one who knows she is beautiful yet does not try to exploit it. Her breasts still rode firmly, each dark aureole a perfect orb, more medallions than objects of passion. She was still naked. It was a nakedness that invited inspection, but not as a thing to be acquired and consumed. Ezekiel looked as one would look at an intricately sculpted vase of thin porcelain.

"Evil to him who thinks evil," thought Ezekiel to himself, quoting an old legal formula.

The road faded and Ezekiel was now standing on the edge of a busy village square. Music, noise and the smell of roasted goat engulfed him. It was night and a huge fire kept shooting sparks heavenward. In the distance, coming toward him, a small procession was making its way slowly through happy villagers. It was a bridal partly. The woman who, minutes ago, had stood naked before him was now adorned like no other virgin bride Ezekiel had ever seen. Beside her stood the Destroyer. Over one shoulder draped the wedding cape he would eventually place on his bride. His face shone. Gone were the fierce eyes and clenched jaw that usually confronted Ezekiel when they met. Instead, the man's head was flung far back as if in perpetual laughter. His delight was palpable and unrestrained. Ezekiel could taste it in his hungry mouth and it was like dark, rich mead.

That is it, thought Ezekiel, watching the Destroyer move leisurely through the throng of well-wishers. *He is without reserve toward her. He holds nothing back.*

It was the wedding Ezekiel wished had been his own, a sprawling extravaganza of sense and feeling. His own had been compressed and muted against the spectre of an approaching Babylonian aggressor.

The bridal group stopped. The Destroyer faced the woman and readied the cape for her shoulders. With its removal from his shoulder, the man's familiar golden frame emerged. The radiance of it framed the woman. Ezekiel heard the covenant: "From now on nobody but myself shall cover thee." And they were gone, into the night.

Ezekiel followed but it was into his own wedding chamber he entered. There was Shaheena, trembling in front of him. His own body quivered as their wedding clothes loosed and they fell to the low couch prepared for them. Tears of longing streamed down as the scene dissolved. When would the Destroyer leave him in peace once and for all?

It was bright sunlight and the streets of whatever city he was now in were filled with the bustle of trade. At first he did not understand the gestures of the woman who blocked his path, for it was neither the time nor place for whores to be working. He froze, or thought he did. She moved on, giving him a lewd wink. Her scent was strong and cheap. He watched her deliberately bump into a merchant whose face marked him for an Egyptian. The proposition was accepted and they entered a narrow doorway nearby. Moments later, or so it seemed, the Egyptian reappeared, still adjusting his clothing. The woman followed soon after, eyes assessing the street.

She is searching for her next customer. There was open carnal desire smeared across her face.

She would lift her skirts to anyone. She has to have them between her legs, he thought. He watched her lead another foreign merchant back through the crowd. The trader cupped her buttocks[18] as they walked, and Ezekiel noticed how she set herself against the pressure of his hand, inviting the public flirtation to continue.

The scene dissolved into a dingy room. Ezekiel was pressed against a wall, elevated, although what his feet touched he did not know. The woman lay on a large packing crate. Around her ranged four men in various stages of undress. She was naked again. Her stomach hung loosely and shifted with every twisted response. The men stood close, penetrating her in several places. The grunts of animals in feral heat were all around him. The room smelled of spent seed.

But there was something about the scene that did not look right. It took Ezekiel some time before he realized what it was. *This is for her satisfaction, not theirs,* he concluded. *She is a whore, yet she is the aggressor.*

A furnace door opened beside him. He turned. The Destroyer had joined him, looking down at the salacious maelstrom. He spoke and his jaw was as tight as ever:

"That is my bride you see before you, son of man. That is my wedding cape she uses as a rag to clean the seed from her crotch. And you ask me if I have a right to be angry?"

Ezekiel was reduced to a rattling whisper. The Destroyer's body was almost white in its heat. His features receded to shifting lines in the brilliance. Ezekiel fell to the ground, groveling at the hem of fiery skirt. "O Sovereign Lord, will you destroy everything? Is there no room for mercy?"

"And if I showed mercy on my people, son of man, would they thank me? No. They would seize my compassion as their eternal right. They have twisted my covenants into a mantra of protection. It does no good to show them mercy. They are beyond that."

"Have you no compassion, O Sovereign Lord?"

"What I have, O son of man, is great pain."

"Pain?"

"You think it is a feeling that is beneath the Master of the Universe? You think it is only reserved for the dust of Adam?"

Ezekiel did not reply. He remained where he was, prostrate and mute.

"Son of man."

"Your servant."

"All these years I have bound your tongue except in my service. It has been a hardship for you, has it not?"

Ezekiel thought about all the things he had wanted to tell people. He thought about Sarah, who was growing up with a silent father. He thought about Shaheena, who could only guess at his inner turmoil.

"Yes, O Sovereign Lord, it has been a great hardship."

"Suffering in silence is a double burden. However, you, O son of man, you have seen my anger. Now you will feel my pain. From you I do not withhold myself. Then, perhaps you will understand."

"Feel your pain?" Ezekiel became rigid. He did not understand. He did not want to understand. But he knew he was being warned. Some greater horror awaited him.

"Yes, son of man. To you will I reveal my innermost thoughts."

When Ezekiel finally lifted his head, he was staring out onto the flat tranquil surface of the Euphrates. The visitation had ended.

———

To Baruch, son of Neriah, living at Jerusalem, from Shaheena, his daughter, wife of Ezekiel, among the exiles at Chebar, near Babylon.

Father, my heart is heavy for you and I tremble for your welfare. It is common news among us that your viceroy, Zedekiah, seeks independence from Nebuchadnezzar and looks to Egypt for protection. Here a great army is being marshaled. Huge food supplies are packaged for the caravans that go both in advance and behind the main army. Nebuchadnezzar prepares a campaign into the eastern crescent to confront the Egyptians once more. You tell me you are safe, yet I ask with timid hope if you will come. Forgive the foolish fears of a weak daughter, Father.

Ezekiel withdraws into himself more each day. It is his frantic despair that touches me. If I understood better all that he sees, then perhaps that knowledge would give me a tranquillity of mind to meet the stress of his fits. But I am left only with his intense, crazed anxiety. It is like some invisible aura creeps stealthily toward me. I feel its approach through my husband, yet I do not comprehend it. These past weeks he has taken to rising each morning and drawing two lines on my forehead with ashes of the fire.[19] Sarah, too, receives a mark. Only then am I free to leave the house. He gazes at me intensely as I leave, and if I do not return at the precise hour I have said, he grows agitated. Once, for no reason at all, he ran to me while I was in the far section of our gardens. At night, his eyes never leave me as I go about making the evening meal. When we lie together there is fierceness to his embrace. It is as if he were trying to draw my soul into his own. His protection smothers me and leaves me frightened more than comforted. It is not from him that I fear harm. Indeed our love for each other is sweet. Nevertheless, the dread or terror that he wrestles with, like Jacob, goes through him and touches me. We are both vulnerable—like strays from the herd that the shepherd has abandoned.

I have written more than I should and I am shamed by my own selfishness. Forgive the tears that cause a blemish on the page. They will irritate the scribe in you, but the father in you will understand. Do not come. Even to write my fears is to make them fade.

By MY OWN HAND, SHAHEENA.

Shaheena folded the letter carefully, got up from the table and placed it in the writing kit. There were others like it already inside. She would not send them. There was no point.

———

To Jeremiah, prophet of Yahweh at Jerusalem, from Ezekiel prophet of Yahweh at Babylon.

Would that I did not have to write and say that Shaheena has died. My mind is still unstable so that I cannot trust myself to write to Baruch. You must tell him for me. It is a cowardly request perhaps, but I know you will do it with gentleness. There are letters here for him that Shaheena did not send. I think I shall not send them.

Like a bright flower I could stare at in wonder each day—perfection in the midst of a falling down world—that was Shaheena. I felt she had been given to me especially by Yahweh as a balm for the stripes I also received from his hand. Now there is nothing left but a patch of soft earth that I do not think will be protected long. Decay is rapid in this land.

Jeremiah, if only she had died by some natural pestilence or accident, I think I could accept the loss. Everything living must die; it is the way God has made it. But Shaheena died at the hand of Yahweh, struck down in a single day, this jewel that was the delight of my eye. And the agony was that he gave me prescience of his intentions.[20]

I pled with the Sovereign Lord to spare her. I marked her forehead but not my own. Her last morning she did not rise from her bed—"a little weariness" was what she said. "Go about your business and I shall be well by evening." I knew otherwise. I kissed her, smoothed the coverlet and stroked her hair. Whatever little rite of endearment I thought of, I did, until she finally turned from me to sleep. Did Yahweh not see how much I loved her? Would his heart not be moved?

By evening a fever had seized her so that she did not know me. I sat, her head in my lap, a cold rag pressed to her forehead. I sat that way until she died.

There is worse. Yahweh has constrained my mourning. It is another pantomime to show that none will mourn when Jerusalem falls. There is no respite from the demands he makes of me. Even my grief is pillaged.

What have I done to deserve the punishment of knowing the future? What did Shaheena do save the mistake of joining her life to mine? All this time I had taken comfort that we, here, were safe. Was I that proud of my own cleverness that Yahweh had to strike? These are the thoughts for which there are no answers. They race madly round my loins. For once, I am glad of the continuing silence imposed on me. Else I would rage against—against I know not what or whom. He said he would show me his pain. He has always spoken truth.

However, I write only of the loss of one person and soon, if you and I are right, the great judgement will begin on your city, on all of us. That you have not already come here to safety tells me that you, like me, have been restrained. May Yahweh deal with you more favourably than is my portion here in Babylon.

By my own hand, Ezekiel.

Epilogue

Ezekiel's speech would remain hindered for seven years. Only when a messenger arrived with news that Jerusalem had fallen was he able to speak normally again.

Endnotes

[1] Ezekiel's wife is never named. This name is fictional.

[2] Jeremiah 27:2 refers to a meeting of ambassadors from the states of Edom, Moab, Ammon, Tyre and Sidon. Coordinated resistance to Nebuchadnezzar never occurred. Some scholars believe that the intrigue was discovered. The discovery would explain why Zedekiah was summoned to Babylon shortly thereafter.

[3] In fact his name was Zedekiah, the same as the regent king of Jerusalem. It was a common name and substituted here so as not to needlessly confuse the reader.

[4] Jeremiah 29:3: Two couriers were sent: Elasah, son of Shaphan, and Gemariah, son of Hilkiah. Both men came from families who were loyal to Yahweh. Shaphan had been the chief executive to Josiah during his reforms, and Hilkiah was the high priest who supervised the temple refurbishment. The verse in Jeremiah also suggests that the couriers carried documents from King Zedekiah, presumably to Nebuchadnezzar. Some historians theorize that his intrigue with the five other local sovereigns had been discovered and that he was sending letters of explanation. In any event it would seem that when it came to finding people who were trustworthy, Zedekiah fell back on those who were loyal Yahwists but not necessarily sympathetic to his policies.

[5] The complete letter may be found in Jeremiah 29.

[6] Ezekiel 3:15 implies that this first vision experienced by Ezekiel included a seven-day "sojourn" into some other community of Jews, at a place called Tel Aviv, near the Kebar river.

[7] Ezekiel 3:24 promises that Ezekiel would be bound by his own people for a time. No context is given.

[8] Ezekiel 4: 1-3 gives the details for Ezekiel's model. The context of the passage is that Yahweh directed the entire event.

[9] Ezekiel 5:1-5: There was a gap of time between when Ezekiel shaved himself and when he finally disposed of the three satchels of hair. One he burned, one he cut up with a short sword, and one he scattered in the wind. The drama was to indicate the fate of Jerusalem's people. Ezekiel was, however, instructed to place a few hairs inside his belt, for safekeeping. See also Isaiah 7:20

[10] Ezekiel 4: 12-15: In fact, Yahweh had originally ordered Ezekiel to use human excrement as fuel. When Ezekiel protested on ceremonial grounds, Yahweh relented.

[11] Ezekiel 1:1ff and elsewhere in this book. Sometimes referred to as cherubim, these creatures appeared frequently in Ezekiel's visions. Their description takes up 21 verses in the first chapter. Ezekiel himself seems to have struggled to describe them with any kind of precision.

[12] Ezekiel 21:18ff. In the original, Nebuchadnezzar, with his advancing army, stopped at this junction and sought various omens to determine which of the two regions he should invade. The dating of this is thought to be 589 BC. Jerusalem fell in July of 587.

[13] Ezekiel 8:16

[14] Ezekiel 9:8; also in 11:13. In both instances, the text reads "Then I fell face-down, crying out...."

[15] Ezekiel 9:6

[16] Ezekiel 12:2

[17] The vision is recorded in Ezekiel 16:1ff. It remains among the more graphic prophecies in the scriptures.

[18] An allusion to Ezekiel 23:3. The full verse reads, "In [Egypt] their breasts were fondled and their virgin bosoms caressed."

[19] Ezekiel 9:4ff speak of Yahweh's scribe preceding the six executioners through the Jerusalem streets. The scribe placed a mark on the foreheads of those who would be spared. Those who received the mark were not killed. The story forms part of a vision Ezekiel would have received before his wife died.

[20] Ezekiel 24:15-18: The original text reads as follows: "The word of the LORD came to me: 'Son of man, with one blow I am about to take away from you the delight of your eyes. Yet do not lament or weep or shed any tears. Groan quietly; do not mourn for the dead. Keep your turban fastened and your sandals on your feet; do not cover the lower part of your face or eat the customary food of mourners.' So I spoke to the people in the morning, and in the evening my wife died. The next morning I did as I had been commanded.

Saving Jeremiah

I t all started when I got the letter from Babylon. I did not recognize the inscription on the packet: "To Ebed-Melech, chief steward in the Royal Household, at Jerusalem, from Belteshazarr, a servant of Nebuchadnezzar." I hefted the flattened bulk of papyri, the edges folded in toward each other and held with a large glob of clay and tallow. The insignia pressed into the clay bulla was an ornate declaration of Babylonian officialdom.

Now how would an official in Babylon even know that a black-faced eunuch slave existed here in Jerusalem, much less write to him? I wondered. Getting the letter was not good news. I was sure that Zedekiah, my king, was already aware that his chief steward had received a private communiqué from the Babylonian court. It was a serious thing to bypass the official political channels, at least from my perspective. And who was Belteshazzar anyway?

I waved away the slave who delivered it and made an obvious show of stuffing it carelessly into the folds of my belt so that a tip of it could still be seen. I had no secrets was what I wanted to advertise. I continued on my way through the private quarters of the palace. Hamutal, the queen mother, had summoned me. Not even a message from Nebuchadnezzar would divert me from that interview. Zedekiah might be king, but Hamutal ruled too, if you get my meaning. She hoarded power like some men hoard gold.

I entered her personal chambers. She was still at toilet, helped by two young slaves. The queen was half-naked and made no effort toward modesty. It is an accepted fact that a eunuch can see everything; after all, we're not *men*. That's why we're given such intimate places of trust within royal households.

She's still beautiful, although she works harder at it these days, I thought. I coughed slightly to signify my presence.

"Lucacia did not please the king last night," Hamutal began. "He was made to look foolish and inadequate."

"She remains in seclusion with her shame," I replied, "under the guard of my own servant." I spoke the truth. Lucacia had come directly to me from Zedekiah's bed and told me the details of their failure. All the girls talked to me. I was safe. Lucacia had been upset. She was a concubine from Tyre, a city well known for its sophisticated concupiscence. She was both diligent and expert in performing her duties.

"This has not happened before. He was simply too besotted to concentrate," she told me. "In the end he fell asleep."

"I was already on my way to the kitchen when you summoned me," I answered. "Last night our king was served a sauce spiced with mudar. The plant is well known in Egypt—an excellent flavouring, but with certain somnolent side effects. It will not be used again.

"You will reassure Zedekiah that he was not to blame?"

"I shall inform the king in such a way that his dignity will not disturbed," I answered. "Leave it with me." We looked hard at each other. She did not believe the spice story. But the kitchen servants reported to me and knew enough to take the blame if asked. Besides, I had been sired in the dark regions of Ethiopia and trained at the Egyptian court. I spoke four languages and was something of a physician. The mystique of being all-knowing was something I carefully guarded. She was from a rude collection of huts called Libnah,[1] close to our western frontier. When it came to identifying an obscure spice, she would not press a conflict.

With my every step along the corridor, the papyri pressed into the rolls of fat that shifted constantly when I walked. I had long since abandoned any attempts at moderation where food was concerned. Some of "us" remained thin; most did not. Life had to have some compensating pleasures.

Zedekiah sat at one end of a long table in the small chamber he used as a day office. King Zedekiah, the twenty-second king to sit on David's throne. But he was not really our king. His nephew, Jehoiachin, the rightful heir, was a hostage in Babylon. Nebuchadnezzar had marched on our city some tens years earlier and Jehoiachin had wisely surrendered. It had been a prudent piece of statesmanship for someone who was only eighteen at the time. Nebuchadnezzar had spared our city. Instead he merely plundered about half the temple treasury and shipped it back to Babylon along with three thousand of our most talented citizens. Jehoiachin and his family were the prime hostages.

In Jehoiachin's stead, Nebuchadnezzar had appointed his uncle, Zedekiah, but only as regent. Zedekiah was himself only twenty-one. So far, he had faithfully collected the annual tribute on behalf of our Babylonian masters. We called him "King" of course. But news from Babylon was that Jehoiachin was alive and prosperous,[2] and this created a certain tentativeness at our court. And receiving a private but official letter from Nebuchadnezzar's court left me open to charges of intrigue.

Inside the chamber a half-dozen men stood posed about the edges of the room. They stood well back from the table in a practised state of relaxed attentiveness. Irijah, captain of palace security, stood behind the king's chair, no more than an arm's length. Sleep still clung to the king's blotchy face. His eyes were slightly puffed.

He has one murderous hangover, I thought. Jonathan, his chief secretary, stood by his side talking in a measured monotone. This was not the morning for loud debates or complex deliberations. Zedekiah grunted at me by way of acknowledgement. I bowed low and found a spot along the wall.

"What is it you want?" he finally growled.

"Only to satisfy my eyes that you are in good health and be granted your pardon."

"Pardon?"

"A certain spice used in last night's dinner—one of the cooks mistakenly used it, not knowing that it encourages a soporific state. Lesser men might still be asleep. But you, I see, have been blessed with the fortitude of a bull. May your god be praised."

Just the flicker of relief crossed his face. If I hadn't been watching him intently, I wouldn't have seen it. *He has been worried,* I concluded, *and will accept this excuse without reflection.*

"See that it does not happen again." He turned back to Jonathan for the next piece of business. I left, bowing obsequiously. One more domestic crisis dealt with. Child's play. Where would kings be were it not for the servants who managed them?

Now to find out who Belteshazzar was and what he wanted with a rotund eunuch living in Jerusalem. I closeted myself in my quarters with orders not to be disturbed. I broke the seal, unfolded the papyri and began to read.

> To Ebed-Melech, chief steward to Zedekiah who reigns in Jerusalem at the pleasure of Nebuchadnezzar, from Belteshazzar, satrap for the province of Nippur and servant to Nebuchadnezzar:
>
> Greetings and may all be well with the household you watch over.
>
> You will not know me by my Babylonian name, given when I joined Nebuchadnezzar's court. But you will surely remember me as Daniel, on whom you showed favour while I attended the academy in Jerusalem …

Daniel! Of course I remembered him. He was by far the brightest student among those destined for positions in the court bureaucracy. There had been four young men who hung together,[3] but Daniel was the leader. They had been among the three thousand deportees. I wasn't surprised that Daniel was now a satrap. His kind were like cream that rose to the top of whatever political stew into which they were tossed.

> … I write to you of a personal matter, and in confidence. It would serve no purpose to advertise that I have been made a eunuch.[4] It was part of my initiation into those closest to the king. My friends, Hananiah, Mishael and Azariah have also received similar treatment and enjoy a corresponding authority as a consequence. Here, amidst the diversity, there is no shame to be "marked." Nebuchadnezzar embraces the best from all the nations he rules and the prevailing perception is that eunuchs focus with great singularity on their responsibilities. As a Jew, however, I grieve that never again can I enter the temple. Two deft cuts of a knife have severed me from far more than my manhood. Yahweh has such a stern code.[5] Even though it has been a year since my castration, there are still certain disturbing sensations about which I seek your advice. My position and, yes, my vanity prevents me

from being too open with others here that have the same
condition ...

My heart went out to this Daniel-cum-Belteshazzar. It had been
easier for me; I had been castrated before puberty in deliberate
preparation for my vocation. I knew that those who lost their testicles
as adults faced far more difficult adjustments. I was lucky. I had no
memory of what it was to be a man. Daniel's letter went on, faltering,
groping for polite speech to describe intimate discomforts. Worst was
the sensation that your testes were still in their sac, swaying against
your thighs. And while Daniel did not mention it specifically, I knew
he would be constantly bothered by the total disconnect between what
his eyes desired and his loins could not register.

We are a strange guild—we who are no longer men. It is a fraternity
that supersedes the households we serve. Our kings might be at war and
we would not betray them. We have no common god. We adopt the
customs and mannerisms of whatever ethnic group we serve. But we
have all lost hope of children, of progeny through which we would live
forever. That is a hardship more profound than sexual pleasures denied.
From what I have observed, sex is vastly overrated. It is the knowledge
that we can never leave behind proof of our ever having lived; that is
the bond that binds us together.

I felt sorry in particular for Daniel. His god, Yahweh, placed such
emphasis on a man's seed. The Jews cut the foreskins from their male-
children at birth. I thought of it as a kind of inaugural blood libation
that marked the seed as the holy property of Yahweh. I wrote him back
that same day with all manner of solicitous advice and sent several
types of creams with the courier. It was the beginning of an enduring
friendship.

———

The political question of our day was how long Nebuchadnezzar
could control us. His hold over Palestine was not absolute and it was
impossible to permanently support his army so far from home. The only
other power of any consequence left in our world was Egypt. If we
allied ourselves with Egypt, and together could defeat Nebuchadnezzar,

we would be independent. There had been a few battles already and Egypt was pushed back to her borders. But I'd been trained in Memphis. Egypt had huge resources and the loss of thirty or forty thousand troops was a mere flesh wound to them. Memphis is one hundred miles from us. Babylon is one thousand. For the moment, we sent tribute to Babylon but ambassadors to Egypt. I think Zedekiah thought himself sly and sophisticated. From where I watched, he looked more like a marionette engaged in a grotesque dance, having his strings pulled in all directions.

I sympathized with Zedekiah's dilemma—to a point. His father, Josiah, had not paid tribute to anyone, and died defending Jewish independence.[6] It was a heritage Zedekiah wished he could emulate. And he craved the good opinions of those around him.

"Nebuchadnezzar cannot sustain control of our territory," they said. "Egypt will push him back to the far side of the Euphrates. Better to assist in the task." "Do you want to be remembered only as Nebuchadnezzar's lap dog?" "Be guided by the memory of your father." The arguments were fierce, unremitting and utterly fallacious. Our best courtiers were gone, hostages to Babylon. Those who rushed to fill the empty chairs had been passed over in first instance for good reason. They were incompetent, and their advice was self-serving. In better times the chaos would have been comical. Now it was pathetic.

It was none of my business, of course. My opinion wasn't sought and I am much too smart to have offered one. But if you want to know the truth, I will tell you. The real issue that lay like a rotting corpse in our midst had nothing to do with King Nebuchadnezzar or Pharaoh Hophra. What really shaped people's counsel was that they did not want King Jehoiachin and the other three thousand hostages to ever return. Having expropriated the exiles' houses, land and palace positions, none of the current crop of courtiers wanted to see the exiles come home. The goblet of affluence had been seized, and there would be no returning it to its former owners. The palace game of my hour was Jew betraying Jew.

A kind of permanent double-speak settled into the court argot. The public hope was for the demise of Babylon and safe return of the Jewish brothers. The private objective was to make sure they never saw their homeland again. And for that to happen there could be no cooperation with Nebuchadnezzar. The motives at court were as black as my skin, and just as pervasive. Zedekiah was no match for such prurient ambition. It took a few years—and, I might add, half our inventory of wine—for him to screw up his courage, but in the end, he finally rebelled and stopped sending the tribute. It was a decision that sealed the fate of the hostages. Only crusty old curmudgeons like Jeremiah objected.

———

The first time I met Jeremiah I thought he was a slop carrier. He was wandering the halls of the palace, looking vacant and lost. Resting on the back of his neck, extending well past both shoulders, was an iron yoke with a broad leather strap hanging from each end. We met in a narrow hallway and I had to manoeuvre my bulk past the tips of his yolk. Something about his posture made me pause. He had already started to pivot sideways, in deference to me, but the end of his ungainly equipment hit the wall, making him wince at the impact. Even through his tunic I could see he was bony. *The yoke must hurt him terribly*, I thought.

"You are looking for the kitchen," I said. It was a statement. "I will take you." I was headed that way myself. It is the accepted custom that menials who clean the palace can eat a meal.

"I was in search of Zedekiah."

I looked at him intently. He didn't look threatening, but neither did he look entirely normal. Intelligence and breeding were obvious in his face. I put my face close to his chest. His clothes had none of the telltale stains and odors that were the occupational badges of those who emptied our latrines. I glanced at his hands. They were large, with long fingers, but smooth and soft. He was no slop carrier.

"Has the king sent for you?" I asked.

"No."

"Does he know you?"

"Yes."

"Who are you?"

"Just a messenger."

99

I couldn't decide if he was being unintentionally obtuse or deliberately insolent. He seemed to be fighting hard to control himself, not trusting his voice to anything beyond one syllable. "Even messengers have to eat," I said finally. "Come with me."

He ate, sitting on a low stool in one corner of the kitchen. The yoke remained on his shoulders. He fell to his food with energy but even in his haste he ate with the mannerisms of a highborn citizen. I stood a short distance away, studying him.

"What is your guild?" I asked. The fright was receding from his eyes and his speech was easier.

"I am a prophet. My father is Buzi. My home is Anathoth." A pause, then, "You are Ebed-Melech, purchased from Pharaoh's court twenty years ago. I remember."

"And you," I threw back, "are Jeremiah."

He grinned sheepishly, then resumed eating, talking between bites. "I was in distress when we first met. A small disagreement on the temple steps left me ... distracted. How did you know my name?"

"Who in Jerusalem has not heard of the prophet from Anathoth who speaks in the name of your god Yahweh?" Jeremiah smiled again. It reminded me of a small child taking delight on receiving a present. There was such a frank innocence about him.

"You are too kind. Who in Jerusalem has not heard of the prophet of Anathoth who lives like an irritating flea in the ear of the king, who harasses the royal household with unending impertinence? That was what you meant to say!"

He was right. It was my turn to smile. "I have received many instructions regarding you, but regrettably they contradict each other.

"Oh?" Jeremiah had finished eating.

"From the king, I have been told to turn you away—but with gentleness. From Irijah, captain of the guard, I am to seize you at once and call him. The queen mother keeps changing her mind. Why, I'm not sure. I have heard you called a traitor in the pay of Babylon, a demented fool, an embarrassment to your guild, and also a holy man who speaks in the name of your unseen god with powerful prescience. Most would have you killed, or at least put away. Some revere you. And all parties ply the king with their opinions." By the time I had finished, he was beaming, nodding his head eagerly at each accusation.

"Yet here you are," I probed, "fresh from trespassing, and masquerading as a hod carrier, lurking through the palace corridors. I could have you imprisoned myself." My voice suggested that I would not. In truth, the man fascinated me. He was nothing as I imagined he might be. His hands were constantly in motion, like independent creatures. He was thin and angular. There was nothing commanding about him. His reputation, or at least the trouble he stirred, up was ten times larger than the man himself.

"Not a hod carrier, surely," he answered. "This is my yoke of bondage." He caressed the end of the metal shaft. "It is really just a stage prop. Hananiah broke the first one I made. It was wooden. This one will last."

I knew Hananiah. He was fat, like me, and came frequently to the king's table. We had exchanged culinary pleasantries. I knew him to be glib, full of optimism and well liked. He too was a prophet.

"And may a humble servant of the king enquire what you did or said to ruffle the otherwise affable Hananiah?"

"I said that he would die before the year was out for having uttered falsehoods in the name of Yahweh. He proclaimed that we would be freed from the Babylonians within two years—an end to paying tribute. But this," Jeremiah stroked his iron bar gently, "this is Babylon. And this," he said, rubbing his red-raw neck, "is us. For seventy years we shall wear their shackles and send them tribute. If we do not, Nebuchadnezzar will destroy us utterly. The temple will be burned and the priests slaughtered like so many sacrifices."

"So says Yahweh—the unseen god of Judah?" It was the only prophetic formula I knew. Prophets were peculiar to the Jews. Re, the god I worshipped, had no such fanatics.

"So says Yahweh."

"And you have come to proclaim this maledictory tidbit to our king?"

Jeremiah emitted a quiet chuckle. "Actually I came hoping for sanctuary. In a strange way, the king is fond of me. And just at present Pashur and his crowd are mad enough to kill me." Pashur was head of the temple guild, second only to the high priest, Zephaniah. Pashur did not take kindly to people who challenged his fiefdom.

"Lucky for you it was me you bumped into and not Irijah. He likes you no better than Pashur does. I will show you a private door that leads into a side street. Best to go home for a time. And please," I added, "take that silly contraption off your shoulders."

Irijah confronted me within the hour. He was at least six feet and a half feet tall. When I say "confronted," I am sincere.

"Jeremiah was in the palace and you did not detain him." Irijah did not waste energy on salutations.

"You have the king's warrant to arrest him? Yet you did not advise the king's household retainers?"

Irijah softened slightly. "I thought we had an understanding."

"We do. We look to the welfare of the king. In matters of security, treason, malfeasance, peculation or sedition, you are supreme. In matters of feeding a harmless holy man with household leftovers, I humbly preside. Besides, you had ample opportunity to arrest him in public at the temple, yet you did not. Why should I think you had changed your mind?"

He glowered at me. It was a stalemate. Zedekiah had not ordered Jeremiah's seizure and whatever had happened at the temple, it had not been grounds for arrest. Murder, perhaps, but not a trial.

"If he comes again," Irijah growled, "see that you inform me."

"Both you and the king shall learn of it at once," I said smoothly. Irijah's dislike of me wasn't personal. He didn't like anyone. A lefthander, superb with a short sword, with the intelligence just above that of an ox, and features to match, he was ideally suited to his job. He saw the world as one large conspiracy. I think his picture of a perfect world was one where everyone was incarcerated. "When in doubt, lock them up" was his watchword.

But boundaries of influence had to be preserved. Until I got the nod from Zedekiah, or perhaps Hamutal, I wasn't going to be cowed. On the other hand, Jeremiah had been arrested twice before on charges of treason. There had not been enough concrete evidence, only fomented proclamations about their god being angry and vengeful. Perhaps he was a traitor in the pay of Babylon. Fortunately for me, it really wasn't that important.

———

When Hananiah was discovered dead in his bed six weeks later I waited for Jeremiah to be elevated to god-like status. There had been no signs of a struggle and no wounds. Hananiah had retired to his chambers the night before, his usual complaisant personage, and just died. It was a powerful omen. But nothing was made of it!

I couldn't recall any magic nearly this potent being worked in Egypt. There, speaking for Re or Aten, Jeremiah would have immediately been promoted to a senior seer. He would have stood close to the pharaoh, the quiet voice behind the throne. Now, that is a country that takes their gods and their gods' messengers seriously.

I could not understand how a people could treat their own holy men—and the god he spoke for—with such contemptuous indifference. In the face of such authentication, I would have expected people to hang on every oracle that Jeremiah uttered. I've worshipped Re all my life and will until the day I die. He is the god allotted me and I have no complaints. But when Hananiah died, I confess I was envious. This Yahweh god, now, he was a god that paid attention to you. But at court it was as if nothing had happened. And Jeremiah had sat in my kitchen!

I wrote to Daniel with the news. Couriers were still travelling between our cities, although their fees had trebled. Our confidences by this time were intimate. I like to think I had become a sort of pseudo father to him. I told him of my astonishment at the wholesale denial of such a powerful omen. Daniel wrote back with even more perturbing news.

MY COLLEAGUE:

I am glad you have knowledge of Jeremiah. He is known here to Nebuchadnezzar's seers and diviners. I do not think it is just because he publicly advocates surrendering to us. There is a Yahweh prophet who lives among us here. Ezekiel is his name. He is given to outrageous dementia and hallucinations, which are taken here as certain signs of his legitimacy. He too prophesies that your city's rebellion will end in its destruction. Even more,

Yahweh himself is in alliance with our god Marduk. At least that is the impression in Nebuchadnezzar's mind.

Nebuchadnezzar is privy to Jeremiah's letter sent to the exiles here. He paid great attention to Jeremiah's oracle promising seventy years of servitude in Babylon.[7] His own diviners were quick to point out that it meant that in his lifetime, at least, Babylon would remain triumphant. So great is the esteem for Jeremiah that our king has ordered his general, Nebuzaradan, to spare Jeremiah's life when Jerusalem is finally subdued.[8]

Nebuzaradan is in overall command of the campaign against your city. Already the siege towers have been dismantled for transport. The main army will leave shortly. Nebuzaradan is a seasoned battle commander. You will know him by a long, ugly scar that starts high on his forehead, descending past his left eye. I give you these markings because there is no doubt here that your city will not withstand the siege. No other city has, and others have been larger.

I wish I had better news to send, but I do not think that Nebuchadnezzar's impending attack will be a surprise to you. The usual strategy is to intimidate his enemies with news of his preparations. I tell you no more than is already public. Nebuchadnezzar does not come in stealth. Perhaps, in Yahweh's mercy, it will be a speedy conquest. Better yet, Zedekiah might surrender before too many of your citizens die.

Was Daniel trying to tell me something apart from the obvious? I wasn't sure.

———

Jerusalem is shaped like a soup ladle. The north end is wider, and beyond the wall is flat farmland. But to the east and south the land drops away suddenly into two steep, narrow valleys. Their sides are rocky and drop quickly almost one hundred feet to the narrow gorge floors. Beyond this valley, on the east, running parallel to our city wall, is a summit ridge we call the Mount of Olives. From its top you can see right into our city. The land to our west is criss-crossed with gulches, steep ridges and hills. There are few roads through it and most of it is good only for grazing. When we are attacked, it is always from the north.

Irijah's face glowed when the Babylonians started to encamp. At last, here was an enemy—brilliantly visible. It never occurred to him that our entire city had become one large jailhouse. A forest of tents grew quickly on our northern side, the first line starting comfortably out of arrow range. Elsewhere around our perimeter we saw signs that the Babylonians had dug in. A small group of tents straddled the top of the Mount of Olives where a signalling platform had been erected. The tents were meant to be visible. It was effective intimidation. I remember the first time I walked the wall and saw that we were totally blockaded. It felt as if a thick rope had encircled my neck. It wasn't tight yet, but little by little it would constrict, like a snake slowly squeezing the life out of a rodent until its eyes popped and ribs cracked like dry sticks. My breath came in hot gasps thinking about it.

Irijah and other military officers showed an avid, almost morbid interest in the details of each day's activities. Despite my fear, I found that I too could not keep away from the wall. Irijah never tired of explaining each development to me.

"In this siege," he told me one day when we met on the battlement, "we hold the advantage."

"How can you tell?" I asked.

"The ravines to our east and south have the effect of doubling our wall height. The valley sides are rock. Tunnelling is not possible from those sides."

"Tunnelling?"

Irijah looked at me as if I was mildly retarded. "Sappers. It's how Ninevah was breached. They used a Hittite corps of engineers and dug toward the base of the wall where the foundations were weakest. Then they excavated under the wall, shoring up the site with timbers. After they were finished, they filled the cavity with straw and branches and set the whole thing afire. The wood burns. The walls collapse. The assault troops rush in. It's simple. It is also the fastest plan of attack. Only a few months of digging are required."

"Will they do that to us?"

"Not likely. Our west flank is vulnerable to sappers but the terrain is too rugged for support troops to easily storm the breach. And siege towers cannot be moved into place. No, it is only our north wall that will be attacked. It allows us to concentrate our defences in only a small section of the perimeter."

"How soon will they attack?" At any moment I expected a wave of foot soldiers to come charging towards us, but what exactly I thought they might do once they reached the base of our walls, I wasn't sure.

Irijah gave a shrug. "Six months, a year. Perhaps never, if their field rations run low. They have a thousand-mile supply chain and probably fifty thousand troops to support. It's the commissariats that really win sieges, not the generals."

The shock I felt must have showed on my face. "A year?" The implications of living cheek to jowl with twenty-five thousand people in space that normally housed only half that number were not pleasant.

"Be glad you are fat." He grinned at me. "You will be half your size before this is over. Besides," he continued, as if he knew what was running through my head, "the city will not always be as crowded. People will start to die soon enough. Tightly penned animals always do. We are no different.

"How will they try to attack us?" I asked.

"Another day, Ebed-Melech. We have lots of time for conversations."

Irijah was right. Time was about the only thing we had in abundance. And filling it with things that boosted our morale became an essential part of our defence. Zedekiah devised a daily routine that kept him both public and accessible. It was not the time for recriminations against those who had counseled that Nebuchadnezzar would not attack us. Instead, we talked loudly about Egypt's army that, no doubt, was already marching to our aid. Until they came, our whole city would suffer together.

Zedekiah made daily inspections of the wall. Our city walls were about twenty feet wide at the top and fifty feet thick at the base. The combined perimeter was just less than eight thousand feet. Along the top, a continuous promenade allowed troops to shift positions quickly. By each gate we had built at least one taller structure that cantilevered slightly beyond the wall. It afforded a good platform from which to shoot at anyone attempting to storm our gates. From its openings, our troops could also shoot at any attackers brave enough to use scaling ladders.

Zedekiah also presided each morning over the city's judiciary. In an open square, just inside the Sheep Gate built into our northern wall, he would sit on a raised dais and receive petitions, settle disputes and dispense punishment. Justice, or at least its external trappings, was part of our public entertainment. The sessions were well attended and fractious. Public justice, open to every citizen, was a tradition that was older than the throne itself. It had its variant form in every town and village throughout our land. When the king did not preside himself, a council of "elders" served as magistrates. It wasn't a perfect system, but it held our worst aggressions in check.

Zedekiah had selected the Sheep Gate deliberately for this daily office. Sometimes you could hear the noise of the Babylonians through the thick walls. It was Zedekiah's way of declaring he would not be cowed.

The palace adopted rationing early. My chief preoccupation became the management of food supplies. I did not change menus at first but started with regulating the amount of food allotted to each meal. By about the fifth month, however, I concluded that fresh meat was too extravagant. I had the livestock butchered and dried the meat.

At first our straitened diet was a novelty. My own modest contribution to our city's weal was to declare a contest for the best stew that could be made from ten ounces of dried goat and six ounces of grain. I set up long trestles in the courtyard and cajoled thirty palace functionaries to preside as judges. But eventually the spices ran low and the meat got tougher. Novelty turned to indifference and in turn to disdain. That was still in the early stages—the first year of siege. I speak of the times when we still had food to complain about.

Outside our walls we watched as the Babylonians assembled their war machines. Irijah explained them to me.

"The tallest ones are portable towers. They will roll these to within arrow range to try to clear the archers off of our walls so that ramparts can be constructed. He pointed to three locations where earth was being systematically heaped to form elevated roadways that would eventually connect to the top of our walls. I could see, however, that it would take months before the roads would be anywhere close to completed.

Irijah pointed to what looked like an oversized harvest wagon covered with a canopy. From one end a stout timber protruded, like an ugly phallus poking its head through a ripped tunic. "That," he said, "is a battering ram. One will be pushed up each rampart to bash the upper section of our walls. The ram pivots on chains and the men who swing it back and forth into our walls stay protected by the hides stretched on the overhead frame. At least that is the theory," he finished with a wolfish grin.

"What do we do in retaliation?" I asked

"To start with, we shoot fire arrows into the hide. If the hide catches, the smoke drives the men away. Then they must wait until dark to retrieve the ram, make repairs and push it up the rampart once more. It is a game that can last for weeks. If they get quite close, we will drop stones directly down in hopes of smashing it altogether. Eventually, however, our walls can be broken."

I retreated to my simple duties of rationing the day's grain and supervising the bakers.

The longer the siege, the more devout people became to the gods they worshipped. Yahweh, the national god, presided over the only temple our city had. Shrines and altars to other deities could be found, but it was only the priests of Yahweh who received royal patronage. The worse things got, the more we looked to Yahweh to save us. After all, that was his job, and Jewish history was full of some spectacular empyrean interventions. I did not hold out much help that Re would intervene on my behalf. Nonetheless, I was as devout as anyone else.

When Zephaniah, the high priest, arrived at court with Pashur I knew something big was imminent. The two men were known not to agree on anything. Zephaniah had a solid reputation for doing the best he could in the midst of chaos. Pashur was a self-serving weasel. By the time the two men had been escorted to the king's day room, I had invented an excuse to be there too.

"May it please the king to hear that sacrifices continue to be offered daily for the salvation of the city," began Zephaniah. His broad, open face wore a permanent look of harried concern.

"You have the only livestock remaining in the city." Zedekiah was in no mood for pious platitudes. "I hope Yahweh is appreciative."

"We believe," continued Zephaniah, "that Yahweh ignores our plight because we have breached our covenant obligations in certain matters."

"Which are?" the king pressed.

"In particular, O king, that most of the leading families in our city continue to impress fellow Jews as slaves. The law of Moses is clear and immutable. Jews can be indentured to other Jews only with consent, and then only for six years. After that, all debts are to be forgiven and freedoms restored. Yet throughout the city, Jew enslaves Jew. It is an offence to our god—at least that is our belief at the temple."

Pashur could wait no longer. "It is not only an offence. These people cannot help but long for their freedom. There is potential for treason, or at least for undermining our defences.

"What is your scheme?" asked Zedekiah coldly.

"That you declare a solemn day of covenant renewal; that you preside over a public ceremony of fidelity to Yahweh and that the ceremony culminates with your proclamation that all Jewish slaves within the city be released," Zephaniah answered. I could see him picturing the event as he spoke.

"And you believe this will move Yahweh sufficiently to help us—this public act of contrition?"

"I do."

"Besides," added Pashur, "the longer the siege, the more important our city's solidarity. Why cultivate malcontents when there is no great benefit achieved?"

"Ebed-Melech," Zedekiah suddenly shouted. "Where is Ebed-Melech?"

"Yours to command," I responded, emerging from the most distant corner of the room.

"Melech, how many Jewish slaves serve at the palace?"

"About twenty," I answered, "plus three of your concubines, of course." I didn't bother to name them. He knew each of them quite well.

"Do the laws of Moses apply to both male and female slaves?" he asked.

"Yes."

Irijah spoke up. "This plan has merit. The total number of male Jewish slaves might be as much as four hundred. They would prove useful in our defence."

"It would require the approval of my advisors," Zedekiah postured.

Jonathan had been waiting his turn. I was intrigued that everyone else in the room except the king had seemed to know about this plan before hand. "I have already made discreet inquiries among the more senior advisors. They will follow your lead in this matter."

Zedekiah turned to me again. "Will the service within my household suffer overly?"

"You will not miss them, I promise. The concubines may choose to remain of their own will."

He breathed out through his nose loudly. It was decision time. The whole room knew it, yet for all that, it was obvious that the poor man could not commit himself. He turned back to Zephaniah.

"Have any of the prophets received oracles concerning this? Is Yahweh's response certain?"

Zephaniah finally let his desperation show. "My king, your city grows more nervous with each day. Who knows for certain the mind of Yahweh? We have been led astray before by oracles that proved calumnious. Surely it can do no harm to do the will of Yahweh in such an obvious matter. To continue in our prayers and sacrifices knowing we are in error is to invite his retribution, not his protection."

"Has Jeremiah spoken of this thing?"

Pashur broke in. "We do not consult those who have already declared themselves friends of Babylon."

"But he is also a friend of Yahweh," said Zedekiah icily. "And Hananiah is no longer with us to consult in this matter." This point hit home.

"Jeremiah has received no special word on this plan," Zedekiah said. I spoke with him directly. Believe me, I would not hide his words, no matter how unwelcome they might be. I too, have a great need to know the mind of Yahweh."

"What is the mood of Jeremiah these days?" asked the king. nonchalantly, as if to give himself time to think.

"Jeremiah remains consistent. He urges a speedy surrender to Nebuchadnezzar. Yahweh has ordained that we will be subjugated to Babylon, voluntarily or otherwise."

"He abuses the free speech we so liberally grant prophets," growled Irijah. "I still believe him to be in the pay of the Babylonians."

"And we await the proofs of your persuasion," Zedekiah replied. "Until then, he will be tolerated." He turned back to Zephaniah. "We shall proceed as you suggest. Make the arrangements. Surely Yahweh will look favourably on such costly penance."

I was pleased with the decision. The Jewish slaves were a collective hard luck story who had indentured themselves as a last desperate measure to stave off a family tragedy of some kind or other. Their stories differed only in the ugly details of lives filled with suffering.

Zedekiah had been long in his cups by the time he summoned me to his chambers. But his mood was rosy.

"Ebed-Melech," he gushed and actually went so far as to put his hand on my shoulder, "I have come to an important decision."

I waited. My face tried to match his happy grin, but I felt idiotic, like someone laughing at a joke he did not hear.

"I am going to include you among the slaves who will shortly be freed. A gift from your king in gratitude for your faithful service to his family." Zedekiah beamed at me, thoroughly pleased at the largesse of the moment.

"My king." I did not know what else to say. Finally, "But it was only meant to apply to Jewish slaves. You are certain in this decision? Some within your court might not be so magnanimous."

"Am I king for nothing?" he crowed. " I free those whom I choose, just as I imprison those whom I choose. And you I choose to free."

It was delightful news and I fell to my knees in genuine thanksgiving. Zedekiah helped me to my feet, pleased that I was so visibly taken in by his pronouncement. Free. I had lived in a world where the word was irrelevant, where it could not attach itself to any concrete event or activity. It didn't matter if Zedekiah was probably indulging himself in the whim of the moment and that nothing would really change. In a few moments I would pledge my continued service to his family and to the court as a token of my gratitude. I knew that Zedekiah not only expected the offer, but also would accept my pledge of renewed fealty with reciprocal farce. I was past the age when I could seriously contemplate any other life than the one for which I had been trained. My station within the court was not without status and authority. But just to be able to walk the city wall, look out to where the hills met the sky and know that I could go there if I wanted to—the thought spread through me like spring flowers overtaking a field against the receding winter snow.

Free. I could remove the large disc that distended my right ear lobe. The hole left behind would never heal, but the dangling ringlet of skin would be a powerful witness to my good fortune. Zedekiah stood close to me, his face still radiating his own satisfaction at his gift. It had been a grand and royal gesture.

Thus I was included in the list of slaves whose names were read aloud in an elaborate rite of public flagellation. I didn't go to the event. Yahweh wasn't my god. Nonetheless, I was grateful in the way a person is grateful when they receive a generous gift from someone who lives far away. But who to thank? This was a Jewish matter and Re had had many years to engineer my freedom if that had been his design. Tentatively, I offered prayers to Yahweh. Not in public of course, and I am embarrassed to admit I included prayers to Yahweh at the same time as my daily office to Re. I never told anyone, and no doubt any good Jew would have been scandalized. But the wine of thanksgiving must have out or it sours; and I poured out my overflowing heart as best I could.

Far be it for me to decipher the mind of Yahweh. My own god, Re, is enough of an inscrutable mystery. But a month after the slaves were freed, Nebuchadnezzar lifted the blockade. Pharaoh Hophra was finally advancing out of Egypt and the Babylonians mobilized their troops and marched south, past our city, to engage the Egyptians in more open territory. Enough troops stayed behind to protect their siege weapons and baggage against any raids from our own meagre militia.

A comfortable stalemate ensued while everyone waited for news from the conflagration to the south. Couriers were allowed access to the city. I received letters from Daniel and sent long, gossipy replies immediately. The Babylonian troops made no effort to molest those citizens who chose to leave our city. Many people did and, from all reports, retained their liberty. It was sound tactics to show kindness to those who left. Of all the siege strategies the Babylonians employed, this civility infuriated Irijah the most. For over a year now we had imagined the noose of foreign hordes as dark savages, eager to strangle us at first sight. Their actions now said otherwise. Our city's destruction was nothing but a professional necessity to be concluded with as little waste as possible. For every person who left was one less person to defend our walls should the siege resume in earnest. Irijah's only solace was that our remaining food stocks would last that much longer.

Jeremiah sought to leave the city and it proved to be his undoing. Irijah kept close and personal watch on who came and went through the city gates.

"What is your business outside the city?" he demanded when he spotted Jeremiah making his way toward the Benjamin gate.

"I go to the property inherited from my father, in Anathoth. You know the place well enough. Three miles to the north."

"Yes, I know it well. It is in the thick of where the Babylonians are encamped. Your own words expose you for the traitor you are."

"Anathoth is my home," protested Jeremiah. " I have no duties that keep me in Jerusalem. And you yourself have made it clear that I am unwelcome at court."

"You are going to report on our city's defences and its food reserves."

"Preposterous!" retorted Jeremiah. But his voice betrayed just how badly he wanted to leave. "Your paranoia has consumed you and you see spies everywhere." Jeremiah's voice was now at full volume, as if hoping to shout himself past this last obstacle.

"Prove to me that you are not a spy," Irijah shouted back. "You, who prophesy victory over us at the hands of Babylon."

"I am a prophet. No one denies it. Not even you. It is my right to proclaim the future. It is more than my right, it is my duty. It is not my fault that the future is not to your liking." His voice was tinged with hysteria.

"You are going over to the Babylonians."

"That's not true. You prevent me from leaving out of personal malice."

But by this time, Jeremiah was being roughly hauled through the crowd and hustled out of sight by several of Irijah's guard. "Place him in custody," shouted Irijah to Jeremiah's retreating back. "He is guilty of treason. Hold him within Jonathan's house. We will get the truth from him quickly enough."

The house belonging to Jonathan, chief executive to the king, had been commandeered by the military. Its upper rooms housed senior officers. Its cellar was both a prison and interrogation room. Rumour was that those who were incarcerated did not live overly long—and those who did wished that they did not. Visitors were discouraged.

———

"Ebed-Melech, I have sorry news." Zedekiah had summoned me again for a private conversation. I did not reply. There was a thin line of sweat lying just at the top of his beard. He did not look directly at me.

This man is frightened, I thought.

"Ebed-Melech, the council has concluded that granting freedom to the Jewish slaves was rash and reckless. We have observed that many are still without homes or the means to support themselves. Now that our city is no longer bottled up, restoring the former order of things is thought to be in the best interests of public order. Tomorrow each family will reclaim their property. The deeds of freedom will be revoked. Life will go back to the way it was."[9]

Zedekiah delivered this long, lame bit of folderol to a spot on the wall three feet to the right of where I stood. My head rejected what my bowels immediately perceived. I was about to be enslaved again. I heard my voice, usually honeyed and unctuous, croak out the question: "Am I included in the decision of the council?"

"It could not be otherwise," he answered. "There can be no exceptions, no favouritism."

My body had forsaken me. I was aware only that I wanted to pee very badly. My groin spasmed and contracted as I fought to control myself. The effort saved me from saying something rash.

"You are my king, yours to command. The welfare of your household remains my unceasing duty."

Only then did Zedekiah look at me. It was the anxious face of a child who knows he has done wrong, yet seeks acceptance despite his actions.

"I cannot stand against my advisors in this affair," he whimpered. "It is not just the loss of property. Seeing their former slaves walking around Jerusalem, free to go where they want—it makes them jealous. They cannot abide their joy."

Ever so cautiously I touched the sleeve of my king. It was a high risk to be so familiar, yet he was so pitifully undone. "I will set an example for others to follow. Your own slaves will not protest. I will see to that."

"You are a loyal servant, Ebed-Melech. I will not forget. Someday you will make a request of me and I will grant it." Somehow I left the room with dignity and fled in haste to the latrine.

I had never even gotten outside the palace walls. The cruelty of it all—like parading fresh, hot bread before the nose of a beggar, only to snatch it back just as he stretches out his hand. But there was nothing to be done. Or so I thought.

Less than two weeks after our conversation, Nebuchadnezzar resumed his blockade. As best as we could gauge from the vantage of our walls, his army hadn't suffered any injury. *So much for our Egyptian allies. They have scampered back to safety.*

Our food supplies had not been replenished during the hiatus. It wasn't harvest time. Twenty feet of stone was now all that separated us from the world's most powerful army. Fear blew through our city like a cold wind, extinguishing the candles of hope.

The public face of the court was brazen optimism. We had no need for others to help us! Nebuchadnezzar's siege army would break themselves against the iron resistance of the Jews. Self-reliance became our mantra. By our own strength we would extricate ourselves from the clutches of Babylon. We had to believe this dogma. The only alternative was unconditional surrender. For most of the court, surrender promised only a summary execution. Nebuchadnezzar would make the leaders pay for such a prolonged gesture of impudence.

Nevertheless, I was not really surprised when Zedekiah sent me to fetch Jeremiah for a private audience. Religion is frequently a good substitute for courage. I found Jeremiah in a tiny cell, resting on a pallet of stinking straw.

"You have become a hod carrier after all, judging from the smell of you," I said lightly. "A sorry spectacle you are."

"It's true." Jeremiah tried to banter in return. "Both my body and my oracles are now equally offensive to the noses of the new illuminati." He could not stand without help. His left foot was swollen and bent in at an odd angle from his leg. One of his cheeks was a blob of purple and orange. It looked like someone had affixed a rotten plum to the side of his face. When he opened his mouth to speak, I noticed gaps in his teeth where there had been none before.

"You're losing weight," he said, grabbing my shoulder for support. "The siege is a tonic for you. Where are we going?"

"Zedekiah wishes a private word with you. But we will stop first at my chambers and attend to your needs."

I bathed him myself, after first cutting away his clothes. He sat helpless on a squat box, letting me gently soap his skin before rinsing him with warmed water. His frame, thin to begin with, was now emaciated, translucent in its frailty. His ribs showed plainly and around his buttocks the skin was loose. I touched him with great tenderness, all the time murmuring dark and foreign curses at his captors. He let me trim his beard and hair, bind his lame foot in a splint and daub ointment on the offending cheek. Food arrived from the kitchen and he ate, chewing carefully on the good side of his mouth.

"You should not have tried to leave the city," I chided gently. "It was just the excuse Irijah has been waiting for."

"I had to try, Ebed-Melech. Has the blockade resumed?"

"It has. Nebuchadnezzar circles our walls like a lion waiting for an ox to finally die."

"Then we are doomed," he replied. "Yahweh will slaughter even the righteous along with the wicked. I thought to escape—that I would be exempted. But Yahweh, it would seem, will kill even his messengers."

"I do not think so, my friend."

Jeremiah searched my face quizzically. "Has Ebed-Melech now become a prophet too?"

I told him about the letter I had received from Daniel saying that he'd been singled out for protection. I described the Babylonian commander. "His face will look not unlike your own," I quipped.

The news entered Jeremiah like water into a dry sponge. "So," I concluded, "while we wait for our death, you wait for your rescue."

"Nebuchadnezzar himself ordered my protection?" Jeremiah pressed me. "He used my actual name?" I removed the letter from its hiding place and gave it to Jeremiah to read. He handed it back to me when he was finished.

"Burn this and any others like it. They are my execution orders if Pashur or Irijah discover them." I promised I would. He limped a little less as we went to find Zedekiah.

"Jeremiah, a true servant of Yahweh, who does not sell his oracles to his own advantage." Zedekiah was manic in the force of his greeting. Jeremiah bowed awkwardly but said nothing. Zedekiah reverted to a more formal tone.

"I have sent for you to see if Yahweh has revealed his mind to you—if there is a word from Yahweh."

"For you in particular?" Jeremiah asked pointedly.

Zedekiah's posture collapsed instantly. "Yes, for me. I need to know if Yahweh will protect me."

"Yahweh has given me a word for you," began Jeremiah flatly. "His word is that you will be handed over to the king of Babylon."[10] Zedekiah blanched as if he had been slapped full in the face.

"Is there no way out then?"

"Only if you surrender."

"The council would never permit that. The worse it gets, the more they are determined to resist."

"Then they will all die," answered Jeremiah. He seized the silence.

"O king, you know I am being held without trial or even an official accusation. You yourself admit that I speak only truth, however disturbing its implications. Since when has truth become a crime? Ignore me. Dismiss me as a nuisance. But please, do not return me to the house of Jonathan. If you do, I shall die. Surely you would not order my death in such stealth."

"What do you propose?" the king asked. "That I give you a signet ring, clothe you in purple and let you walk the streets under my aegis?"

"I am yours to command, O king. Only please, do not send me back to that prison. I will die."

I cleared my throat. "The palace barracks are secure and well guarded. Yet they are public enough that no harm would come to this man without your order. And as a royal prisoner, Jeremiah could draw rations from your table."

Zedekiah seized on the solution. "It is a good compromise. No one can accuse me of setting you free, yet you will be safe. I shall order your transfer to the barracks." Turning to me he said, "See to his daily food. And take him directly to the barracks commander. Tell him my orders will follow shortly."

I left Jeremiah sitting on a bench in the courtyard the guards used for assembly each morning. Later I would return with a pallet for him to sleep on under one of the covered archways. "I shall bring your food myself," I promised. "It is becoming too valuable a commodity."

———

Irijah's predictions about our cramped quarters proved all too accurate. People began to die in large numbers. At first it was just the very old or the infirm, but all of us were vulnerable. You had only to cough in public to watch people instantly turn their heads and grab for a rag to cover their mouths. Soon entire families were dying from some savage plague that ran through our streets unchallenged. It was a ghastly job to remove the dead. Often it was the smell of decaying bodies, still on their beds and bloated to the bursting point, that led to their discovery. Their neighbours, driven by wild-eyed fear for their own health, would drag out the bodies and dump them over the south wall.

By now I had been forced to reduce rations to about two cups of grain per person each day. It was a third of what we were used to. Elsewhere in the city even this small amount of food was a luxury. Irijah gave me a squad of soldiers to protect our royal supplies. Their presence provided a discipline that sheltered us from the worst of what we would have done to each other.

Outside the palace perimeter the cruel law of the wild mounted the pedestal of power. People slept behind heavily barricaded doors, fearful of being plundered under the cover of night. Even in daylight a harried furtiveness infested our streets. The usual open markets with their loud and protracted arguments over price and quality were replaced by whispered conversations in secluded doorways. The food being sold was never visible. Buyer and seller would disappear into some dark corner and melt away quickly once the exchange had been made.

The children suffered most. They were the most vulnerable in the herd. Usually our streets are full of young gamins living by their wits. They were the first to disappear. Their bodies did not form part of the putrid mound of decomposing flesh that steadily mounted up against our south wall. There was no public discussion. It was as if the children had never existed. But we all knew the truth. A people under siege had become a tribe that ate their young.

The ones who had stooped to cannibalism were easy to identify. They did not grow gaunt and pinched along with the rest of us. Instead, their health and energy were mute accusations of the depravity that ruled their souls. It did not stop with urchins. Babies and toddlers began to vanish from families. I pictured the mothers of these children, hunched over a pot, adding chunks of flesh into a broth.[11] One day earlier, that flesh had been their children. Did they remember the feel of their tiny mouths sucking on their teats? And was it their fathers who had butchered them, or had some dark trade sprung up that would kill and dress young children in exchange for some of the meat?

Zedekiah knew what was going on. He must have known, for Hamutal, his own mother, was among those who did not grow lean. Her good looks were more important. I could forgive my Jewish masters for many things; yes, even for the loss of my freedom. But I would not

119

forgive them for the atrocity against the children. Was it for nothing that this people had so carefully circumcised themselves since the time of Abraham, offering the fruit of their loins back to Yahweh as His own? Nebuchadnezzar had every right to obliterate them from the land. They had ceased to be human. In a crazy way, part of me hoped fervently that they would not surrender.

The more determined the courtiers became in their resistance, the greater my satisfaction. Nebuchadnezzar's anger was growing higher with each passing day. Finally, one day it would leap across the top of our walls and consume us. The men at court seemed blind to the obvious. Each day the ramps edged a little closer to our walls. It would be only a few weeks until the battering rams would be moved into position against the upper walls. Each day we grew a little weaker. But a hysterical, frenzied optimism had gripped the palace so that reason fled. It subsumed the throne. Zedekiah did not so much govern as sit atop a wave of denial that swept away any wiser counsel that might be heard.

––––––

In the eight hundred and fifty-first day of the siege the first battering ram was pushed up its ramp into position. Two mobile towers were wheeled close on its flanks, their upper platforms crammed with archers intent on clearing our walls so that those operating the ram could work unmolested. Three days later a second ram was in position about a hundred yards further along our north wall. The final stages of the siege had begun. Irijah's face, drawn and tense, became a miniature reflection of our enemy's progress.

"How much time left?" I asked him as he hurried through the palace.

"Weeks," was his one-word assessment. I followed him to where Zedekiah and the court were waiting for his report.

"The news?" Zedekiah asked.

"The wall at the first ram remains unbroken as yet. At the second point of attack two stones have been dislodged. The Babylonians have brought up a third tower of archers in support, although its position is not ideal. However, we lose about seven men from active duty each day.

Their archers have an unlimited supply of arrows and shoot two arrows for every one of ours. The heads are new. Nebuchadnezzar has brought a forge with him and can make as many as he needs. I have conscripted citizens to collect those that fall within our walls. Those we shall send back." Irijah gave his report in short, terse sentences. But he managed an ugly grin at his concluding black joke.

"Can we dislodge the rams?" asked Jonathan. " I thought their coverings could be burned."

"Their archers keep us restricted and pinned down. And at night they roll the rams back away from our walls out of range. It is a huge effort each day to haul them back against our walls and I did not think they could do it. They are using a pulley system of some kind and we cannot dislodge the harness they have secured into the base of our walls. This is a new technique."

"What can be done to slow them?" Zedekiah asked. Irijah had obviously been waiting for the question, as he did not hesitate to respond.

"I seek permission to dismantle the western section of the palace quarters, both upper and lower floors.[12] It has the largest timbers and we can use them to buttress the walls. I will hang some of the timbers from ropes so that they rest horizontally on the outside of our wall. The force of the ram will be deflected and not directly absorbed by any one individual stone. I have not seen this done and don't know for certain of its effect. The rest of the timbers I will use to strengthen the interior."

"Would you seek to dismantle the temple as well?" Jonathan asked coldly. It was obvious he did not yet grasp what was happening on the north wall. One or two of the more vocal courtiers laughed but it did not catch on. Irijah turned toward the sound and it ceased abruptly.

"I considered it," he said calmly, "but its cedar is almost five hundred years old, and not as thick. And it would take some time to remove the gold sheathing that encases it." He flung one last sentence into the silence. "Otherwise, yes, I would dismantle it."

"Only half my palace," Zedekiah finally responded. He was trying for a light, brave tone, but the saliva had fled his mouth and the words came out high and cracked. He tried again. "I am fortunate that it does not contain my sleeping quarters or the grand throne room. Tell me, have you any other recommendations for my defence?"

I did not realize until then just how stretched Irijah was or how desperate he felt our situation to be.

"There is."

"What else do you seek?"

"Let me execute Jeremiah!" Irijah's face exploded into naked anger. "It is hard enough that we fight a superior enemy without. Yet, I do that with zeal and loyalty. But you, O King, keep a serpent alive in our midst. I told you of the seven men I lose each day on the north wall. I have not yet told you that I lose another four men over the western wall each night. Daily Jeremiah sits in the barracks and counsels surrender and defection.[13] He promises that the Babylonians will not kill them—that this Yahweh god of his will protect all who surrender just as surely as he will kill all who resist."

"God of ours," interrupted Zedekiah.

"Who cares whose God he is or what the source of his anger?" screamed Irijah into Zedekiah's face. "Jeremiah kills four of your soldiers each night just as surely as if they were shot defending the wall. Yet, you permit him sanctuary. Where is the logic in it?" Irijah stood breathing heavily as if he had just run from the north wall itself. I could see his left eyelid twitching uncontrollably. I surveyed the room. No one would speak against Irijah.

But Pashur saw that Zedekiah could not bring himself to order Jeremiah's death. With his reptilian cunning, he offered the compromise Zedekiah so desperately craved.

"O King, you are right to give pause in a decision so extreme and so final. Who better than a priest could give you counsel where Yahweh is involved? But Irijah's problem is also extreme. I urge you, simply allow us to silence Jeremiah—to render him inaccessible. That will answer Irijah's concerns."

Zedekiah sagged. He would take the easy option.

"Jeremiah is prisoner of the barracks. It is within your jurisdiction to restrain him. Who is the king to interfere in the discipline of a prisoner? And as for your other bold request, Irijah, you may have as much of my palace as you need to keep our city secure." Zedekiah attempted a grand exit through a door behind him, but he looked more like a gopher scurrying into his hole.

Pashur and Irijah left the room together, conferring quietly, no doubt about how to best silence Jeremiah short of a public execution. The morning when I went to deliver Jeremiah's food I discovered their solution. In one corner of the courtyard was an abandoned cistern, used long ago for water. Its bottom was thick, soft mud, not quite quicksand but wet enough that a man would sink slowly into it. It is the kind of bottom that only grips harder the more you struggle to escape its ooze. Jeremiah lay at the bottom of the cistern. He was quite silent.

I lay on my belly—much easier to do these days—with my head peering over the edge of the dry well. He lay awkwardly on his back and his legs appeared amputated at the knees. I pushed my head further into the pit, my eyes adjusting to the gloom. His legs had not been cut off, only buried in the muck so that they bent at right angles at the knees.

"Jeremiah, Jeremiah," I called down softly. My voice seemed to lose its way in the foul air.

"Jeremiah." I tried again. His head moved slightly and he opened his mouth.

"Who is it?" I thought he said.

"Its Ebed-Melech. I've got bread. Can you move your arms to catch it if I toss it to you?"

"Water, I need water."

"I'll fetch it." Taking my sash, I wrapped the small cake so as to protect it from the mud and tossed it as best I could towards his face. I hurried away in search of a water bag and enough string to lower it. By the time I returned, Jeremiah had found the cake but he did not start to eat until half the water was gone.

"Thank you."

A heavy foot connected with my side and I rolled over to stare into a soldier's scowling face. We knew each other slightly. I had been a daily visitor to the barracks.

"What will happen to him?" I asked, still lying on the ground.

"Leave the barracks. Do not return. Jeremiah is no longer your concern or your charge."

I scuttled away without protest and returned to my room. Jeremiah had been left to die. Denied food and water, he would last perhaps three days. It was a solution as quiet as it was cowardly. No one would be responsible. No one could be blamed. In better times there were those within the city who would have protested. But these times were not normal. Fifteen thousand of our citizens were already dead, their bodies heaped at the base of our southern wall with the rest of our garbage. What was one more corpse that would lie at the bottom of a pit? In a few weeks most of us would be dead anyway.

I stared for a long time at the small statue of Re. Yahweh seemed so much more personal, at least the way Jeremiah spoke of him.

Perhaps gods are as different as people, I thought. I tried to imagine what it would be like to receive a visitation from a god—some experience so powerful that I would abandon my own ambition and safety just to proclaim the oracles put into my mouth. I wasn't sure I liked Yahweh just then. I certainly didn't understand his abuse of Jeremiah. Re made no such demands on me for which I was grateful.

But neither does Re speak to me. My future remains precarious and obscure. Jeremiah's god declares the future, both in its glory and in its horror. And it comes to pass. How can the Jews be so indifferent?

It's not indifference, I concluded. *It is depraved stubbornness that refuses to bend to anyone—to Nebuchadnezzar or to their own god. And because they will not submit, they must silence the voice that says they must. What is the point of having such a powerful god if you will not listen to him? Yahweh has cause to be angry. These people are not worthy of him.*

I exhaled loudly and straightened my robes. Some people, when they know they haven't a long time to live, say it doesn't matter what you do. I disagree. When you are down to your last few weeks, it matters very much. Jeremiah would not die, at least not in the bottom of a putrid pit at the hands of his own people. Not for nothing did I know how to manipulate the king.

I waited until mid morning. Zedekiah was at one of the city gates conducting his daily ritual of public justice. The proceedings had long lost their substance but at least it gave the citizens daily proof that their king had not escaped over the wall in the night. The noise of the crowd competed with the shouts of soldiers, the harsh clang of arrows on stones and the steady thud of the ram. It was an absurd setting for the daily charade.

Forcing my way through the small crowd, I began loudly. "O king, a great affront to the throne takes place, even as we speak. There are some in the city that ignore your court and your powers. They take vengeance into their own hands and mock your authority. Even now they are set to kill a man you have declared should live."

"Ebed-Melech, approach my chair and make your petition. Who seeks to challenge me in this way?"

I knew better than to name names. To put blame on Irijah, especially in public, would put the king in an impossible situation. "Certain men have thrown the prophet Jeremiah into a cistern that lies within the barracks. They deprive him of both food and water. It is true that you ordered his detention, but you did not order his death. These men go beyond their authority. They do wrong."

"He is a prisoner. Harsh treatment is to be expected." Zedekiah signaled me wildly with his eyes pleading, "Don't make Jeremiah a public issue. You were there when Irijah made his demands. I am caught. You know this. Don't do this to me." I ignored his eyes.

"A prisoner, yes, but one who is not yet tried, sentenced or even charged. Your orders were for his detention only, to await your future consideration. But these men are intent on killing Jeremiah. Worse, they seek to do it in secret."

"What is it you wish?" Zedekiah asked woodenly.

"That I be granted leave to remove him from the pit; that he be allowed a daily ration, however meagre." And then, leaning forward, I put my mouth very close to Zedekiah's ear and continued softly: "You said, O King, that one day I would come to you with a request, and that you would grant it. Behold, this is that day."

I stepped back and waited. Zedekiah recoiled as if I had punched him in the groin. And in some respects, I had.

"The king's decrees are not to be undermined nor subverted. You have my leave to remove Jeremiah from the cistern and attend to his needs. Even prisoners must know of the king's concern for justice."

It took four of us the best part of an hour to hoist Jeremiah back to solid ground. We threw down bundles of old cloaks I'd taken from a palace wardroom. Jeremiah wrapped these under his armpits so that the ropes would not cut him. He could not stand on his own. Instead, I propped him against a courtyard pillar while I washed him yet again. I told him briefly of what I had done.

"You care for me beyond what is required," he said, "and you risk your own life to save mine. Why?"

I busied myself with a cloth and did not look at him.

"We are alike," I finally answered. "We have no children. Only our deeds will speak for us after we are gone." And ever so carefully, I drew him to my breast.

————

I calculated that we had enough food for only another three weeks and told Zedekiah as much in private.

"Irijah hounds me for a larger share to be given the soldiers. It is obvious they are weak. They tire so quickly he has reduced their daily watch on the wall to only three hours."

"Do not change the allocations," he replied. "It is our walls that we depend on. Even if we were all well nourished, the Babylonians outnumber us badly. If the walls are breached, we are finished."

"I am sorry, my king." And then I added, "It appears our walls will not hold indefinitely."

"Yes, Irijah has said the same to me already."

"Perhaps you and your family should make plans to escape," I ventured. Zedekiah did not reply so I continued. "I shall prepare several sacks of food in case you need to leave in haste."

He did not protest or contradict my suggestion. His thoughts were elsewhere. He said suddenly, "I want to see Jeremiah again. But it must be in private—no one else around. Can you arrange it? Can it be done?"

"Can you not simply send for him?" I answered. "Could you not go to the palace barracks yourself?"

A shameful smile stole across Zedekiah's face. "You do not understand the way things are. Even you have more liberty than I am allowed by my trusted advisors." The last two words were delivered with biting sarcasm. I considered the options and settled on the best plan I could think of.

"Tonight, before sundown, go to the temple by way of its side entrance, as if to offer an evening prayer. I shall bring Jeremiah to the same doorway. I will say that Pashur wishes to question him. The barrack guards will allow it. Jeremiah cannot even walk without help. He could not possibly escape. You can talk in the small portico just outside the door."

"I will be there," answered Zedekiah.

How the mighty have been brought low, I thought, *that the king of Judah must stoop to such deception. He skulks around like a kitchen slave.*

Jeremiah leaned heavily on my shoulder as we approached the temple. Sure enough, Zedekiah was waiting. I eased my friend down so that he sat on the stoop leading up to the door and retired a few paces. Neither man seemed to notice me. Zedekiah spoke first and when he did, it was as if he'd been waiting all his life to begin. The words flew out of his mouth, tumbling over themselves with anxious energy.

"Jeremiah, what is my future? What does Yahweh say? Has he no compassion at all left in him for his people—for me?"

"You will only kill me if I reply," said Jeremiah coldly. " Why should I entice your anger or the rage of your advisors?"

"I swear to you in the name of Yahweh himself, I will not harm you, nor give you to the men who want you killed." Jeremiah did not reply and Zedekiah burst out again. "Jeremiah, please, I beg you, what should I do?"

"Do you really want the truth? Very well, I will tell you what Yahweh paints in my mind so vividly that it blots out all else. I see your concubines being given over to the pleasures of Nebuchadnezzar's officers, where they are used by many. I see your mother, Hamutal, fat from the flesh of infants, lying dead on the ground with her bowels splayed out around her. I see the heads of your sons, eyes still open, staring up at you in accusation that it was you who somehow beheaded them, and not Nebuchadnezzar. I see Pashur, Irijah and the whole sorry host of those you call 'princes' being thrust through with the sword. I see Zephaniah, who even now stands within the temple pleading with Yahweh for mercy—a righteous man if ever there was one—I see him among those who will be executed. And you, O King of Judah, who has the power to erase all that Yahweh puts in my head, I see you with your eye sockets empty, in chains, living out your wretched days with only your memories to visit you."

"Is there no other future that you can see for me?" Zedekiah's voice was a strangled whisper.

"Yes," said Jeremiah, his body tensed forward to give force to his words. "Yes, surrender the city, even now, and you and your family will live. Even now, Yahweh gives you a chance."

"What you ask is impossible."

"It is what Yahweh asks."

"You do not understand. None of you understands. You think it is as simple as opening our gates and parading out to the Babylonians? I haven't the power to do it. I would be restrained by my own advisors. And even if I could, and if Nebuchadnezzar did set me free, what would I be free for? I will tell you! I would be free to be the object of abuse and ridicule by all who have already deserted to his throne. Stripped of all status, how long do you think I would live? No, Jeremiah, the choice you give me is no choice at all. I cannot surrender the city. I will not."

"Then Jerusalem will burn and my vision will come to pass," came the reply. There was nothing more to say. Dusk had settled and it was hard to see their faces. Zedekiah spoke again.

"We have been observed, I am certain, and you will be questioned. Tell no one else of our conversation and you will live. Say only that you pled with me not to be returned to Jonathan's house but to remain in the palace barracks. I shall say the same."

I helped Jeremiah to his feet and plodded slowly back toward the barracks. Jeremiah's breath laboured hot on my neck. But just as we approached the courtyard entrance he chuckled quietly. It was raspy and faint.

"I forgot to tell Zedekiah of one other vision," he said.

"Oh?"

"Yes." He stopped and our faces were almost touching. "I did not tell him that I also saw his household slave Ebed-Melech alive and safe by the hand of Yahweh."

I gulped audibly. "You would not joke about such an oracle?" I pressed him. "And you are sure it was me that you saw in your vision?"

"How many fat, black-faced eunuchs do you think inhabit Jerusalem?" he replied. "Did you think that Yahweh would overlook you?"

"He is not my god."

"I wonder at that."

We had reached the entrance and I left Jeremiah to make his own way to his sleeping pallet. I watched him limp painfully into the darkness. I turned toward my own quarters and settled in to wait. I did not think it would be long.

Epilogue

In the nine hundred and twenty-first day of the siege, the north wall of the city was breached and the city was occupied by Babylonian troops. About a third of the citizens were killed. Zedekiah and his family attempted escape through a postern gate in the east wall the night before the final attack. They were captured close to Jericho and taken to Nebuchadnezzar's campaign headquarters, some sixty miles north of Jerusalem. They were joined by about seventy other officials, received sentencing and were executed. Only Zedekiah was kept alive. His eyes were put out with hot coals. The last thing he saw was the execution of his sons.

Jehoiachin was eventually released from prison in Babylon and spent the remainder of his life as an honoured guest of the king. Not only did Nebuzaradan spare Jeremiah's life, he set him free, giving him food and money. Jeremiah declined an invitation to join Nebuchadnezzar's court, choosing instead to remain with the "poorest of the land who had not been taken into exile" (Jer. 40:7).

Nebuzaradan's assessment of his victory over Jerusalem is recorded in a conversation with Jeremiah:

> "Yahweh, your God pronounced this evil against this
> place; Yahweh has brought it about, and has done as he said.
> Because you sinned against Yahweh, and did not obey his
> voice, this thing has come upon you." (Jer. 40:2,3)

Endnotes

[1] II Kings 23:31

[2] Archeological findings at Babylon include texts that refer to Jehoiachin as "King of Judah" and indicate that he was a pensioner at Nebuchadnezzar's court. As well, a handle from a large wine jar has been discovered in Palestine with the inscription "Eliakim, steward of Jehoiachin." Scholarly opinion is that Jehoiachin retained title to the crown vineyards even while he himself was in Babylon.

[3] Daniel 1:6ff: The three friends were Hananiah, Mishael and Azariah. Their Babylonian names were Shadrach, Meshach and Abednego. Readers may recall a Bible story of how these three men were thrown into a furnace for refusing to worship the pagan idol erected by Nebuchadnezzar. Miraculously, they not only survived, but experienced a supernatural visitation while in the flames. See Daniel chapter 3:1-30 for the story.

[4] Two prophecies clearly foretell that certain Jewish exiles would be made eunuchs and serve in Nebuchadnezzar's administration: Isaiah 39:7 reads "And some of your descendents, your own flesh and blood who will be born to you, will be taken away, and they will become eunuchs in the palace of the king of Babylon." The same words are repeated in II Kings 20:18. Both were proclaimed by the prophet Isaiah about 200 years earlier.

[5] Priests (the Levite tribe) with any kind of physical disability were barred from the temple. Crushed testicles are specifically included in the list of blemishes. Similarly, not even animals that had been castrated could be offered as sacrifices. See Leviticus, chapters 21&22. Daniel's tribe of origin is not recorded.

[6] Josiah died at the age of 32 in a needless battle with Egyptian forces who were seeking safe conduct through Judah's territory en route to attack Nebuchadnezzar.

[7] Jeremiah sent a public letter to the Jews held hostage in Babylon. In it he instructed them to "build houses, plant gardens and take wives, and seek the prosperity of Babylon." It specifically promised that no one would return from Babylon for seventy years. This letter would have been widely circulated and debated. See Jeremiah 29.

[8] Jeremiah 39:11 cites Nebuchadnezzar's command regarding Jeremiah. It is logical to conclude that he would not have been set free without special instructions from the highest authority.

[9] Jeremiah 34:8: Both the freeing of the Jewish slaves and their subsequent re-enslavement triggered an oracle by Jeremiah in which Yahweh promised that the citizens of Jerusalem would also be set "free." In Jeremiah's oracle however, they would be free to the ravages of the sword, pestilence and famine.

[10] Jeremiah 37:17

[11] Lamentations 4:10 reads, "The hands of compassionate women have boiled their own children; they became their food in the destruction of the daughter of my people."

[12] Jeremiah 33:4 reads, "For thus says Yahweh concerning houses of the kings of Judah which were torn down to make a defense against the siege mounds ... I have hidden my face from this city."

[13] Jeremiah 38:2

THE QUEEN OF HEAVEN

Inanna[1] slipped back to her hut just in time to rescue their evening meal from burning. She had taken a chance, leaving this close to supper. Her husband, Johanan, was close by and could easily have noticed her absence. Still, the compulsion for one last prayer and sacrifice—the rites of connecting—before the day ended, won out over her caution. The spot she used wasn't far away—just a cranny in the ravine that hid their camp from view. Moving quickly, she placed the bundle she carried back into its hiding place behind some tall clay jars used to store food. She didn't keep Ishtar's statue in the ravine—it was only a terracotta figurine, easily damaged. Already one of her breasts was chipped. Somehow, knowing the icon was close at hand, though wrapped in rags, gave Inanna a sense of security. These were perilous times and security, even the feeling of it, was not to be trivialized.

Johanan entered. If he had noticed his wife's absence, he did not make it an issue. Her worship of the goddess Ishtar was a long-standing irritation between them. He followed Yahweh, or so he would tell people.

He removed his leather vest and placed his short sword carefully on the earth floor within easy reach. When it was time for sleep he would move it again, close to the straw pallet they shared, and take it out of its sheath. Three years of guerrilla warfare had fostered some strange habits. But he was still alive.

"Is it true?" Inanna asked him as they ate, scanning his face through the receding light.

"I am still not convinced entirely, but for certain the rumour is widespread. Our scouts have not seen Babylonian troops anywhere for the past ten days. Yet Jerusalem still smoulders. If they have truly left our lands, it was not long ago."

"What will you do?" she asked. They finished their meal and sat relaxed in the dark. The ambient heat from the stones of their extinguished cooking fire enveloped Johanan like a hot bath. It was his favourite time of day, when his stomach was full and their one-room hut resisted the night air. For a few minutes he did not have to do anything except sit.

"What will you do?" she asked again.

"We will go," he answered. "We haven't any other real choice in the matter. But only after Mizpah has been well inspected. Tomorrow two of my men will enter the town dressed as farmers." He laughed slightly. "It will not be a hard disguise considering that up until three years ago, that's what they were. And if their eyes confirm the rumour—and the Babylonian troops truly have withdrawn and this is not some clever ruse to lure us into the open—then we shall march to Mizpah and meet our new governor. His name is Gedaliah. We took lessons together a long time ago."

"Peace." She drew the word out long over her tongue. "It has been so long since I have heard the word, let alone know what it might mean."

"It means, my faithful wife, that you will have to leave these opulent surroundings and adjust to the hardships of our two-storey house at Bethlehem." He kissed her on the cheek, leaving his face close. She liked the feel of his beard and liked more the softness of his voice. He was not a professional soldier, only a natural leader shaped by the times.

"But surely I will be allowed to hunch over a badly vented fire each evening and cook the same monotonous broth?" she quipped.

"Only if you insist. Who knows," he continued, "we might even have to put up with a servant once again, and water easily fetched from a well instead of from muddy streams. We might have to endure the feel of soft cotton sleeping linens, cool and clean against our naked bodies. Ah, the tribulations of peace. I can scarcely bear the thought of what awaits us!"

They groped their way to the pallet and pulled a thick shawl over themselves. Their bodies lay close despite their dirt and the smell of dank straw. They fell asleep making up the new "hardships" of peace they would soon experience. But not before Johanan took his sword out of its scabbard. Peace hadn't arrived just yet.

The rumour that filled everyone's head circulated in the form of an invitation for any remaining militia to present themselves at Mizpah for formal decommissioning. There would be no reprisals from Nebuchadnezzar's troops, most of whom had already left the area. Instead, Gedaliah, the regent governor, would receive them honourably and give them leave to resettle within the land. Johanan's regiment numbered about one hundred men.

Several such militia bands had survived, dug into the Palestinian hills, doing what they could to harass the Babylonians during the three-year siege of Jerusalem. Their homes were in hidden enclaves, steep ravines and dried up wadis. They had moved often, dismantling or abandoning their makeshift huts. None of their efforts had affected the outcome of the war. Nebuchadnezzar had arrived from Babylon with almost seventy-five thousand troops and an efficient caravan system to keep them supplied. King Zedekiah, the last of Judah's kings as it turned out, had recklessly rebelled against Nebuchadnezzar, hoping the Egyptian army would march north to his aid. Instead, Jerusalem had been besieged and in the nine hundred and twenty-one days it took to break its walls, more than two-thirds of its citizens had died.

The Babylonians were not barbarians as the Assyrians had been before them. But Nebuchadnezzar had not become ruler of the entire world, save Egypt, by being magnanimous. Like locusts marching steadily through a wheat field, he and his army had systematically stripped Jerusalem bare of all its valuables, torn down huge sections of its walls, broken every gate and then set fire to the entire city. The denuding had taken three months of concentrated effort, overseen by a Babylonian general[2] who specialized in the collection of war prizes and booty. Jerusalem still smouldered. The Yahweh temple in particular still sent up smoke. Cynics among Johanan's men referred to it as the last great burnt offering to Yahweh.

That Gedaliah was simply a governor was the most telling proof of their collective impoverishment. Judah had shrunk from nation to province. There would be no taxes levied. There weren't people enough to properly inhabit the land.

Johanan suspected the rumours were quite true. Already he'd heard that several other regiments had shown themselves. Ishmael, son of Nethaniah, had been the first. Ishmael was not easily tricked. What bothered Johanan most about the rumours was that Ishmael *had* been the first to present himself to Gedaliah. Of all the resistance leaders, Ishmael was the most virulent. It was quite out of character for Ishmael to have embraced peace so easily and so quickly. Ishmael took pleasure in killing. There was a wildness to him that he made no effort to control or conceal. The two men had met a few times but Johanan had steered clear of any coordinated tactics. There was something about Ishmael that was repulsive to Johanan. While the last three years had gradually ground Johanan down in the way sand storms erode rock, Ishmael and the men he commanded remained energetic and daring, as as if they took nourishment from each engagement.

Johanan had not survived these three years by being rash. And when the intelligence he gathered didn't quite fit, he went slowly.

And Ishmael's men have paid dearly for their blood-lust, he thought. *I have twice the men still alive.*

The "farmers" returned from Mizpah and confirmed that indeed the war with Babylon was over.

"I saw only about a dozen of their troops," said one of the spies. "They seem to be advisors more than anything—certainly not the fittest bunch of men Nebuchadnezzar has put in the field."

"What of Gedaliah?" asked Johanan.

"From all reports, he is tireless in his efforts to resettle the land. And there's food to be had," the spy added with hungry eyes. "There are grain fields and vineyards that still produce. Whole sections of farmland are unoccupied. Gedaliah grants title to the properties and settles disputes. But there is more than enough land to go around."

"Then we'll go and present ourselves," Johanan said, loudly enough to be a public announcement. "Fifty of us will march tomorrow. The rest will follow with the families. It's over."

"It's over." People ate the words like honey stumbled upon in the wild. It left a sweet, lingering sensation.

Inanna baked cakes and was generous with her supplies. Some they would eat tonight as part of a camp-wide celebration. But some would be a thank offering for Ishtar.

She did not forsake us, Inanna thought. Her heart seemed to expand in keeping with her cakes. *To be alive, to live a day without looking over my shoulder, jumping at every noise. Thanks be to the one who watched over me.*

The cakes were a flat, dense recipe that she cooked in two large portions on a bronze platter. They would be slightly charred on the bottom.

But Ishtar accepts that I have no baking oven. She is a warrior. However, she is also a woman. She understands these things.

Afterward, while the cakes were still hot, Inanna began to cut the loaves into the shapes of small, rotund people. She made the figures the way her mother had taught her and worked deftly to minimize the trimmings. When she was finished cutting she began to decorate each little figure with dried currents and nuts, chopped fine. Breasts and labia were essential to identify their sex. So, too, was some article of warfare. Inanna traced a crude bow in one of the chubby arms of each little cake-figure. Beyond these three things, the cakes could be as ornate and elaborate as skill and ingredients afforded. *I will do better at Bethlehem,* she promised herself.

That afternoon she took her statue from its hiding place and carried it, together with her cakes, to the hollow in the ravine. She leaned the statue upright and spread four cakes at her base. Sitting down she began her usual prayers of thanks and petitions. She closed her eyes. Inanna was not so stupid as to think the simple clay figure in front of her was actually a deity. Ishtar, if she lived anywhere, kept residence on a star called Venus, the first to show itself each summer evening. The clay "asherah," as the figurines were called—with half a breast chipped off and a base that was unstable—was only the flimsiest of aids to help her focus. Once they had settled again she would find a better icon to replace her current one, something taller and made of bronze.

Three of the cakes she would leave in the ravine. No doubt small rodents came to eat them. It didn't matter. Their essence drifted upward to rejoin with the great source of all nourishment. Today Inanna would make a special offering. After her prayers she took the fourth cake and, breaking it carefully, began to eat it herself. The rites of hospitality were ancient furrows in the earth of civilization and a shared meal was intimate fellowship. She munched the cake deliberately, two women in sympathy with each other, giving and receiving freely.

Ishtar occupied Inanna's mind in many forms, each having its foundation in the ancient dramas of the god world. Just now it was Ishtar the source of love that played in her imagination, but she did not resemble the plump matronly cake shapes in the least. Ishtar was thin and willowy; an impish grin bubbled from the corners of her mouth, and her eyes shone in anticipation of coupling. This was the Ishtar whose essence seeped out of Inanna so that Johanan's entry into her was smooth and pleasant. This was the Ishtar whose breath blew across Inanna's nipples so that she trembled in delight. The Ishtar of passion gave the secret joys of womanhood as early heralds to the mystery of motherhood.

With peace will come children, Inanna thought. Johanan and she had avoided a child these past years and their intimacies had suffered as a result. Into their sex had crept a calculated restraint that frustrated them both. It would change now and Inanna sat transfixed in gratitude for the gifts Ishtar now offered. She pictured Johanan erupting inside of her, with Ishtar, the impish grin still visible, hovering above their bed. *His seed is gift to you*, the image said. *The waiting is over.*

<hr>

It was impossible not to like Gedaliah, son of Ahikam, grandson of Shaphan. This wasn't just the easy confidence of someone whose lineage was both well known and respected. He was handsome and kept his face free of hair, and the result was a youth that belied his age. He was not the most intelligent of persons, but he made up for it by intensely focusing on what was at hand, and he lived comfortably both with what he was and was not. When he listened, the whole universe shrank to the person in front of him.

For the past three generations family members had filled senior positions at court. Their deep and abiding devotion to Yahweh was public knowledge. There had been times when Yahweh worship had been politically unpopular, yet the clan's devotion to the Jewish god was as steadfast as their loyalty to the monarchy, regardless of who sat on the throne. His father, Ahikam, had been the public defender of the prophet Jeremiah, saving him from execution. Duplicity was not in their vocabulary, and as a result they were given positions of great trust. How Gedaliah had escaped the fate of most of the other court officials remained a mystery. Most had been quickly tried and executed by the Babylonians. Nevertheless, Gedaliah's family's reputation for integrity must have become known to Nebuchadnezzar, whose practice it was to appoint local governors whenever possible.

"Welcome, Johanan, it's been a long time," shouted Gedaliah as he rushed into the town square to embrace his childhood friend. "I heard the most terrible of rumours—that you'd been wounded in an ambush."

"Your servant at last." Johanan grinned, all formality gone. "We didn't know who was still alive in Jerusalem until a few weeks ago. Yahweh has watched over you." The two embraced heavily and Gedaliah kept his arm around Johanan's shoulder as he moved through Johanan's men. "You've lost weight," continued Johanan.

"So would you if you had lived three years on siege rations." Gedaliah laughed. "I still dream about food. But you look fit enough for all you've been through. I should have left Jerusalem with you when there was still time for all the good I did trying to persuade Zedekiah to surrender. But what's past is past and can't be changed."

"Is it really true?" Johanan asked softly. "Have the Babylonians really left us in peace?"

Gedaliah stopped and looked squarely into Johanan's face. "It's true. No more occupation. No more reprisals. We will not be molested or disturbed—those who have survived.

"Who else has responded from among the resistance groups? I heard Ishmael has disbanded."

"Come and gone again," confirmed Gedaliah. "He announced he was taking lands to the east—he and most of his men."

"How far east?" Johanan asked casually.

"I'm told he has settled almost at the frontier."

"Where our lands touch on Ammonite territory?"

"Yes. Ishmael won't tolerate their insolence. He'll make a good buffer. One less thing for me to worry about. The last thing we need is to be harassed by King Baalis and his lot."

"Did the Ammonites surrender to Nebuchadnezzar then?" asked Johanan. "I had not heard that."

"Not exactly." Gedaliah's continued light tone sounded evasive. His voice was as transparent as his face. "Their lands are too hilly and their towns too small for Nebuchadnezzar to have wasted his troops. Besides, it's not as if the Ammonites had an army."

"Who else has come in?"

"Seraiah arrived last week. Ephai's two sons are here, but the eldest is badly hurt. Neither of them had many men. And, of course, your brother, Jonathan. He was delighted that he'd beat you in. Still as irrepressible as ever."

A loud shout interrupted Gedaliah. From a doorway sprang a young man, still fumbling with his cloak. "Johanan, Johanan. I've been waiting for you all week." The young man ran headlong into Johanan.

"Jonathan?"

"Didn't think your little brother had what it took to survive, eh?" His brother seized Johanan just below the shoulders and jumped up and down in front of him. Johanan reached to embrace Jonathan, who was more like an excited puppy than a seasoned guerrilla leader.

Johanan started to cry, the big sloppy tears of someone whose nerves have been stretched taut. Gedaliah stepped away, watching the two brothers pummel each other as if to make certain the other was not an apparition, repeating one another's name. Finally Gedaliah said, "Jaazaniah has arrived as well." Neither man paid him any attention.

———

Later that day Johanan and his men formally paraded in front of three grey-haired Babylonians who accepted their garbled pledges of peace with neither praise nor insult. Not even their swords were required.

Are we that beggared a people that even our surrender is without notice? thought Johanan. It was still hard for him to absorb the reality that he and his meagre band of fighters counted for nothing. But at the large table, talking with other leaders, he got some feeling of elation. Sitting safe out of earshot of the Babylonian officers, Johanan was affirmed as a hero and leader.

The next day Gedaliah sent for him. The invitation came with great politeness, but it was a summons all the same.

"Johanan," Gedaliah began once they had seated themselves at opposite sides of a large, imposing table, "rumour, I am certain, has robbed me of anything I could tell you that you have not already heard. It is true that there is much vacant land. People report there is still enough wheat in the fields and olives on the trees that we will not starve. After what most of us have lived on these past years, it feels like a banquet. Tell me where you will settle and I will confer the requisite deeds to your family."

"Bethlehem," Johanan replied quickly. "It's where we had a house before ... before the carnage."

"I will see you are given land in the area," said Gedaliah. "Your men are likewise free to choose. We are a small enough people that I can see each family head in person."

"My king surely has need of some militia, a guard of some sort?"

"Governor," corrected Gedaliah quickly. "The kings are gone. The throne of David is now a war trophy currently stuffed into a baggage cart lumbering toward Babylon." He paused, letting the full force of his words penetrate. Then, more gently, he added, "And without a throne to lose, what need have I for a guard? Johanan, there is no one left to threaten us. We are too few even to quarrel among ourselves over the land. Besides, the Babylonians might interpret the presence of a guard incorrectly."

"What of King Zedekiah? He is still alive, is he not?"

"Alive, with his eyes burned out, chained to some post in Nebuchadnezzar's palace."

"His sons?"

"Their beheading was the last thing Zedekiah saw."

"So what will become of us?" Johanan asked. "Without a king, the Yahweh priests scattered, with the temple reduced to a smoking rubbish heap, eight out of ten of our people either dead or gone ..." He was not a scholar, but even he knew of the dark chaos that had been their lot before the age of kings. "We will not survive as a people," he continued. "Even our God seems to have abandoned us."

Gedaliah reached across the table and touched Johanan's sleeve. "There are some, one at least, who do not think so: Jeremiah, the prophet. He survived the siege and still speaks oracles in the name of Yahweh.

"What would he have us believe?"

"That we have been pruned and cut back but not dug up by the roots. The tree of David will send up new shoots and the throne will not stay empty forever."

"Eloquent enough platitudes. They are what's required to prop us up. Do you think he really hears the words of Yahweh? So many of his kind are deluded, or worse, outright charlatans, singing for their supper."

"I do. Fervently."

"Why?" The question sat between them in the silence that followed. "Why is Jeremiah to be believed?" repeated Johanan. "The same God who takes credit for our destruction now opens his hands towards us? What other god treats his followers so callously?"

"If it's proof you want," began Gedaliah, "go look on the ruins of Jerusalem. Go inhale the smoke of the fires. Jeremiah was the only prophet who predicted it could happen if we did not surrender. Even when he was under arrest for treason, he never changed. I never saw a more fearless man."

"So we go suddenly from Yahweh's punishments to his protection?"

"Is it Jeremiah or the God he speaks for that you doubt? Yahweh is the god allotted us. He has punished. Now he blesses. I cannot explain it, but somehow I feel that I have been called to a great new beginning—to give leadership now, at this time. For this purpose I did not die in the siege and escaped execution by Nebuchadnezzar. Somehow, I am part of Yahweh's plan to build us up once more. And if not Yahweh, what do you propose? To abandon the last of your heritage and go worship Molech as the Ammonites do? Or Ishtar?"

Keep my wife out of this, Johanan thought hotly. *What she does to make sense of this crazy world is her own business.* Gedaliah had cut to what mattered most: Was Yahweh still in charge? And if so, where exactly was he now that his temple had been destroyed?

"Where is Jeremiah at present?" asked Johanan.

"At Anathoth,[3] about six miles north of Jerusalem."

"You gave him land?"

"Actually, I didn't. He already held title to his cousin's farm. Right at the height of the siege, when Jeremiah was under arrest for treason, he arranged to buy land. Paid top price for it too. The whole thing was some kind of pantomime promising future prosperity. Surprising that the prophet had that kind of money. I suspect that Baruch, Jeremiah's scribe, had a hand in it—his family is wealthy, or at least it was."

"Prophets are a strange lot," murmured Johanan.

Johanan shrugged and stood up. "My sword is yours to command," he said formally. "At present it remains sheathed. But should you ever need its protection, only send the word. You may not be king, and our enemies may have retired from the field. Still," he formed a wry grin, "the lion has not yet lain down with the lamb and I do not think I will grind my sword into a pruning hook just yet." The men grasped each other's forearms in a two-handed embrace across the table.

"Bethlehem is not far from here," said Gedaliah. "Please visit me often."

"Watch your eastern flank," Johanan warned in parting.

Johanan and Inanna's two-storey house at Bethlehem no longer had its roof, but the oven had not been broken and the well water was still fresh. Inanna and Johanan settled in as best they could, along with other Jewish families who had sought the relative safety of neighbouring territories[4] during the Babylonian campaign.

Skilled workers of any kind were in short supply—let along artisans and idol makers. Inanna never did find a replacement for her Ishtar statue. Iron and bronze could not be had. Ploughs, hoes and hammers were now more valuable than swords and shields. Johanan was tempted more than once to transform his sword into something more practical. As it was, he used most of his arrowheads to create a large rude rake with which to start a garden. The land was generous that season and, true to Gedaliah's predictions, they were left undisturbed. Hope had not blossomed into confidence and progress, but at least the seeds had been planted. Still, Johanan kept in touch with his men, as did his brother Jonathan.

It never hurts to be watchful, he thought.

Seraiah, carrying his scarred shield of crocodile hide, rode into Bethlehem bringing news to Johanan. "Ishmael's turned," he began abruptly. "He means to kill Gedaliah. King Baalis of Ammon has offered a huge sum of gold to the person who kills Gedaliah. Ishmael has accepted the contract. Somehow, I do not think it is only the gold that makes him do it."

"How do you know this?" asked Johanan. "Surely secrecy is in his interest if he means to go through with it."

"Ishmael has made it known among the fighting men that the assignment is his alone. I think he means to gauge the mood of the people, to discover the extent of our discontent. Perhaps he hopes others will join his brigade."

"How many men still follow Ishmael?"

"Only ten from what we know."

"Enough to pull it off."

"What do you suggest?" asked Seraiah. Peace or not, Johanan was still the natural leader among the fighting men.

"We ride to Gedaliah. Now. We should take Jonathan with us. Gedaliah will listen better to a delegation." He left the room. When he returned he wore a leather vest. His short sword hung at his waist. "Just like old times, eh, my friends?" His mouth smiled, but his eyes did not.

Treachery from our own kin, he thought. *Is any Jew destined to be allowed to live?*

They reached Mizpah late in the afternoon. Gedaliah saw them at once and listened quietly to the report.

"What you say is not true," he said when they finished.

"You think we have come with lies in our mouths?" retorted Johanan.

"Not at all. Somehow, your intelligence is flawed. Ishmael is headstrong, short tempered and, yes, difficult to reason with. But he is, above all else, Jewish. What sane Jew would risk reprisals from Babylon? It's true that he may be jealous at my appointment, such as it is. But to assassinate me? Never."

"Do not forget that he is a member of the royal family through his mother's side," Jonathan broke in. "Perhaps he sees himself as king."

"With just ten men following? Not even his enormous ego could hide the obvious. The people do not hunger for a king. They hunger for bread and olive oil and mutton. They crave peace. The royal chevron is an anathema for most. Look no further than Jerusalem to see the foolishness of a king's leadership."

"Baalis has never surrendered to the Babylonians. Killing you, their regent, continues the conflict. Ishmael, too, resists peace. From their perspective, you are the traitor, a weasel who profits from collaboration," Jonathan argued.

"Perhaps that is true," replied Gedaliah. "But to kill me is to attack Babylon. What kind of person wages war against Nebuchadnezzar with ten men? Baalis is greedy and clever. Ishmael is hot headed. But neither of them is stupid."

"But maybe they are imbalanced—or wish to die themselves," Jonathan said.

Seraiah spoke up. "Who benefits from this rumour? If everyone suffers from your death, why does this news persist?"

"It is a joke of some kind," replied Gedaliah. "A dark joke, to be sure, and one that already has Jew mistrusting Jew."

"At least let us send you some men as protection," pleaded Johanan.

"It is not necessary," Gedaliah insisted, then indicated that the meeting was clearly over.

The men left.

———

"Gedaliah knows in his gut that the rumour is true," he said to Inanna several nights later as the lay in bed together. "What I can't discern is why he will not respond, or at least let others intervene. Gedaliah's family is not shy about making hard decisions."

"Perhaps he has received an oracle—that he will not be harmed. Jeremiah visits him regularly."

"He would have told us."

"Perhaps he cannot accept that any Jew would stoop to such madness. That man's heart knows no deceit."

"He spent three years witnessing the collective madness of Jerusalem's courtiers. He is not naïve. No, I think you were closer to the mark with your first idea. He believes it is Yahweh's intent to build us up—that the punishment is over. If that is true, then he is safe. And he is too honourable to take pre-emptive action against a rumour."

Inanna looked at her husband closely. There were things they did not agree on. Johanan's ability to sense danger wasn't one of them. It had kept them alive during the past years.

"You believe Ishmael to be a traitor?" she asked softly.

"I do. Gedaliah risks all of our lives by doing nothing. If Ishmael succeeds, do you really think the Babylonians would ignore the challenge to their authority? If we go unpunished, it encourages others to seek independence. And punishment, when it comes, will not stop at just killing one Jew and his ten fanatic followers."

"Then you must act. There is no option. This thing involves all of us."

Johanan sought out Gedaliah once more. They met alone[5] and spoke without reserve.

"You know Ishmael intends to kill you," Johanan began.

"Even if I agreed with you, I cannot arrest a man for his thoughts. Who would be left free?"

"Even if you are not afraid for yourself, surely the welfare of those who still live in the land is worth something."

"What do you suggest I do?"

"You? Nothing. Only rule us wisely and intercede with the Babylonians. But I am freer. Give me leave to kill Ishmael, now, while he is unsuspecting. My brother and I will go. No one will know who actually murdered him."

"Am I to order the death of a Jew?"

"Would you sit idly by and watch us utterly extinguished? Nebuchadnezzar will not tolerate a challenge to his authority. It would not take a large force to kill us all. And even if he did not send an expedition immediately, he would eventually march this way to attack Egypt. It is inevitable."

"Johanan, I have invited Ishmael to visit me."

Johanan's face went white with this news, but before he could speak, Gedaliah continued. "This whole sad rumour must be put to rest.

Peace and reconciliation. That is what must be demonstrated. That is the role to which I have been called. And Ishmael has accepted. He sends the most generous of responses. He is as anxious as I to shake the slander that besmirches his robe."

Every feature in the governor's gaze told him that the decision would not be revisited. "At least let us give you an honour guard," Johanan insisted.

"I will greet Ishmael with an open heart and hands. The presence of a guard only undermines the peace that must be built. Besides, my Babylonian advisors remain with me. They are a huge deterrent and less likely to give offence."

Johanan was speechless. When he could bear the silence no longer, he met Gedaliah's gaze. "Johanan, it is mine to govern us through this tribulation. If you cannot trust in my judgement, at least believe that Yahweh will not permit the further slaughter of his people."

He trusts in Yahweh with the same fervour as Inanna believes that Ishtar watches over us. And what is more, he chooses the shield of an invisible god over my sword. Would that the heavens remained separate from the earth. It would be easier, reflected Johanan bitterly.

———

News of Gedaliah's death ripped through the land like a summer storm. Johanan heard it first from three Jews from the north who stumbled into Bethlehem, their heads and faces were shorn, their clothing plain; they were pious Jews who had come down on a holy pilgrimage to the temple ruins, intent on making an oblation to Yahweh. They were three of a company of eighty, most of whom now lay dead in a dry pit within the walls of Mizpah.

Johanan questioned them deftly, trying to coax the story out in some semblance of order. It was an impossible task. With each new morsel of information, Johanan felt a dense fog closing in around him in ever-thickening whorls. The war years were returning, the years when nothing could be trusted, nothing was stable. He willed himself to remain calm, counting his breaths, forcing his lungs to slow and then expand more fully.

The story that floated in tiny, disconnected facts before him was still largely incomplete, but he knew for certain that a large number of people had been murdered at Mizpah. A man who called himself Ishmael had left the city, forcing about fifty people to march with him.

"How many armed men followed Ishmael?" Johanan asked. The pilgrims were not sure. Fewer than the hostages.

"In what direction did they march?"

"Easterly."

"How long ago did they leave Mizpah?"

"Yesterday morning. They marched slowly. The hostages were tethered together in groups. Some of them were women."

"How did you three come to escape?"

"We rubbed our bindings on a sharp rock all last night and ran off at first light."

It was enough to act on. The rest of the details would have to wait. Johanan, the resistance fighter, was now in full ascendancy. The three pilgrims would wait under guard until he returned. Runners were dispatched to assemble men. It was a call to arms that registered everywhere except in Johanan's heart.

This cannot be. It must not be.

A small group left before sundown, making their way toward Mizpah. More would join them through the night. Inanna watched them leave. Johanan had been so preoccupied that he had not even said goodbye.

Three days later Johanan returned. He appeared at the door of his home and sagged into its frame for support before entering the room.

"We missed Ishmael," he began flatly. "He and eight men made it into Ammonite territory."

Inanna busied herself with food and some flat beer. She knew from past experience that her husband had not yet fully come home but was still playing out the details of the conflict. She did not touch him—time for that later.

"Eat and drink," she said softly. "You need it."

"Begin to pack," he replied. "We leave in the morning. The rest of my men remain with the hostages at Geruth Chimham." She said nothing, careful to show no surprise at this sudden instruction.

"We missed him," Johanan said again. "They had not gotten far. We caught up with them at the Gibeon springs. I was close enough to see his teeth and the insolent bastard sidestepped my thrust and got away. The hostages were milling around like stupid sheep, all tied together with rope. I could not cut my way through them quickly enough. By then, Ishmael was gone."

"Gedaliah?"

"He was at the bottom of a cistern in Mizpah. They put him in first, it would seem. We buried everyone on our way back. Nobody wanted to touch them. It was a gruesome affair and everyone gagged at the stench, sure they were breathing in some savage pestilence. A few of the bodies burst apart under the strain of the ropes we used hauling them out—they had been dead for four days."

Johanan put his heads in his hands, sighed, then continued. "We found the Babylonian officers. We found twenty Jews that the hostages could put names to. A few people remained unnamed. One body I knew."

"Who?" Inanna asked.

"Jonathan. I did not know he'd gone to Mizpah. Three years he endures the worst that Nebuchadnezzar can throw at us, and he survives. And what is it that kills him? A slimy Jewish renegade sitting at the same table with him."

"It was treachery then?"

"Of the worst kind. The hostages we freed filled in the gaps in the pilgrims' story. Oh yes, we buried their seventy-odd friends as well. Theirs were the first bodies we hauled out— the last ones killed, it looked.

"It seems Ishmael arrived at the banquet of peace and reconciliation with ten men. One minute everyone was crammed into long tables, eating and praising the spices used with the rice. The next minute Ishmael and his men pulled out their swords and killed everyone within reach. Then he fanned out through town, closed the gates and penned up whomever he could find. He threw the dead bodies into an abandoned reservoir."

"But the pilgrims?" asked Inanna. "Surely they were not at the banquet."

At the question, Johanan gagged and Inanna moved closer. His throat convulsed as if to dislodge something that had blocked his breath. It was several minutes before Johanan could speak again. He was cross-legged on the floor, leaning forward so that the weight of his body was on his arms. His head hung low and he seemed to be studying the dirt floor. The only sound was his heavy panting. She had to lean forward to catch his words, now directed at the floor in dull short gasps of breath.

"They had not yet arrived in the town. Not until next morning. Ishmael spied them approaching and went out to welcome them. He lauded their devotion and piety. He even cut a small lock of his own hair and tore a bit of his tunic. Said he would go with them himself if he weren't so unworthy. Then, as if the idea has just occurred to him, he said, 'Come and let our Governor, Gedaliah, meet you and bless your sacred journey.'

"No sooner were they inside the gates than Ishmael's men closed in and butchered all but ten. 'Sacred journey,' he'd said to them. Can you believe it?"

"But why?" asked Inanna.

"Because that is Ishmael." Inanna strained to hear her husband's voice. "And I failed to kill him." He continued to sit, hunched forward, looking more like a punished animal than a battle commander. She shifted her position until she could lay one arm across his shoulders. He did not flinch or jump, but neither did he move. Slowly she drew herself closer into an awkward embrace. He remained rigid.

"We leave at first light to rejoin the others. They are waiting for me at Geruth Chimham."

"What will we do?"

"It is not my decision alone to make. By the time this news reaches Babylon, I expect Nebuchadnezzar will hear only that another uprising has occurred among the Jews and that his officers and governor have been murdered. It will be enough to send troops. Kill first and inquire later will be their approach."

"What are the choices?"

"Stay and take our chances. Scatter in all directions. Or head for Egypt—the only land free of Babylonian control."

"For how long?"

The question made him turn around and stare straight at her with the look of a teacher who is incredulous that a child has not comprehended the simplest of lessons.

"For how long?" he repeated. "Forever."

———

Johanan slept the sleep of one who has not seen rest for several days. But for Inanna there was no such sanctuary. Restless, she got up and padded softly to the main room. She lit one tiny oil lamp that, in the absolute darkness of the house, played freely over the walls. It was not a strong light. She sat for a while. The light was a small bird, loosed from its cage, flitting about the room, short dabs of yellow light quickly swallowed by shadow only to reappear somewhere else in the next instant.

Finally she went to her hiding place and removed Ishtar, placing the disfigured icon on the table, close to the lamp. For all her scars, the lumpy clay figure stood solid and comforting against the blackness that ringed her. Inanna pictured Ishtar in her war garb.

You have suffered with us, she thought, *but you are not defeated. You have not left us.*

Johanan entered. She could hear his breathing but could only faintly see his form as he stood in the opening that connected to their sleeping room. She did not turn and made no effort to rise and hide the terracotta asherah. Caught between her husband and her god, she stayed fixed, waiting for Johanan's burst of irritation. Instead, he continued to stand silently. His breathing still carried the effects of sleep.

"You still take comfort in gazing at childhood toys." He made no move toward the statue or her.

I will not fight him, but neither will I withdraw, she thought.

"The adoration of Yahweh requires more from those who follow him. Without an image to focus the mind, it is more difficult to connect. I have great respect for his adherents. But Ishtar, too, is an ancient goddess. Different. That is all." It was old ground she was covering and in that there was safety.

"Yahweh seems far removed just now." This was a huge concession for him to voice. "It's strange, but when I found the body of my brother,

153

I felt relief of some kind. For all these years of fighting I have lived waiting for the news of his death, expecting to die myself at any time. Fighting the Babylonians to keep our people free was such a clear and unfettered ambition. Those who died at least died in the hope that the battle was not over. There was something noble, or at least purposeful, in what we did. I like to think he might have struck out at least once before Ishmael got him. It is a lucky thing to die with hope and purpose still in your chest. But to live now—it is a great punishment."

"And you, my husband-warrior, carry a great many people on your shoulders."

"Yes." Johanan's mind wandered to what awaited him the next day. He could see the drained, anxious faces that would turn toward him as he entered the camp. "What is the plan?" they would ask. "Which way to safety?" For three years he had accepted the responsibility willingly enough, devised the attacks, found safe camps. It was not fair that he should have to continue. All he wanted to do was rest. It was such a small desire. Even that had been taken away from him.

"I am thinking," he began slowly, "of seeking out the prophet they call Jeremiah. He speaks oracles in the name of Yahweh. He spoke accurately enough during the siege. The people would take great comfort in a word from Yahweh." He exhaled in a long, loud sigh. "So would I."

This thing is too big for him, thought Inanna. *In all the years of fighting he never sought an omen, followed only his common sense. But finally a thing confronts him that he cannot master and he seeks the heavens.*

A mixture of great sympathy and elation filled Inanna's heart.

"Where is he?" she asked.

"Oh, close enough. Anathoth. It's an hour's walk."

She was silent and he felt her disapproval through it.

"You think this is a foolish thing? I stand here in the presence of your god meekly enough. Yet you think searching out Yahweh's mouthpiece is a vain waste of time?"

"Any contact with the heavens is not to be scorned," she answered.

"But what?"

154

"But even if you were given a word of promise—that Yahweh's host of angels would surround us—would you rely on it?"

"So you think Jeremiah would deceive us?"

"Not at all. Sometimes, Johanan, the gods seem unable to help, however much they might wish to. I do not understand it. But the evidence confronts us at every turn."

"You mean the pilgrims?"

She had not thought of them, but saw instantly where his mind had traveled.

"Their death seems especially cruel," she answered.

"I know what you mean. Through all these years of fighting I have carried a kind of tally sheet, keeping a rough ranking of who most or least deserved to live. It was my way of making sense of the randomness. But if ever anyone deserved our God's protection, those seventy pilgrims did. Jonathan, the others, even Gedaliah, we are all soiled with the ugly residue of doing what had to be done to survive. But the pilgrims ..." Johanan left the protest unfinished.

"Do not seek out Jeremiah," Inanna said. "I know it is not my place to counsel you on a question you have not asked, but I am filled with great unease about the matter.

"Is it because I seek Yahweh's voice and not Ishtar's?"

"My husband, all these years, I have asked her to watch over you, to be at your side each time you left our camps. And she heard my poor petitions. Never have I said a word of scorn against Yahweh. I cannot say what has happened. But Yahweh is not with us."

"He has abandoned us?"

"I know only that our fidelity is no longer practical. It has not been for some time. Continuing in the Yahweh customs—where has it gotten us?"

"Do you think gods can die?" Johanan asked quietly. Inanna could hardly believe he had voiced such a daring question, or that he would ask it of her.

He is staggering under his load.

"The old stories are filled with such events," she answered evenly. "I do believe that there are certain gods for certain times. And since you have asked me frankly, I will tell you, however much it pains me to say it: I do not believe this is Yahweh's time."

Not until they were back on their bed, waiting for sleep, did Inanna remember that she had left Ishtar on the table.

——————

Johanan did seek out Jeremiah. What was more, he took a willing delegation from the camp.

I am not the only one who requires an omen, he thought.

Jeremiah seemed to be expecting them, for he was sitting on a stool in the town square. Beside him stood a younger man with a proprietorial scowl on his face. Unlike Jeremiah, whose long straight hair hung white to his shoulders, his younger assistant was quite bald. Only a curly beard trimmed into a point remained.

This must be Baruch, thought Johanan

"We come in search of wisdom," he began. He bent, deferentially, wondering if he should kneel?

The two men, entirely surrounded, eyed each other carefully, keenly aware of the public scrutiny within which they would have to talk. Jeremiah held a walking stick and, even on the stool, leaned into it slightly. Johanan had expected a more imposing figure. Instead he stared down at a slight man, lost in a too-big robe, with oversized hands that ended in wrists as thin as a child's. His eyes might have been kind, but they receded behind an ugly welt that ran across his cheekbone. It ended just at the edge of his right eye, where the flesh was puffy, tinged with purple and yellow.

He has been horribly beaten, thought Johanan as he studied Jeremiah. *No wonder his servant is so protective.*

"You would be Johanan." Jeremiah spoke mildly. "Your brother was Jonathan. I am sorry." A pause, and then he continued. "It is strange that we have not met before. There are so few of us left."

"You were confined at Jerusalem," ventured Johanan. " I was at large."

"Yes, I had the privilege of a wall between myself and the Babylonians, unlike yourself. News of your bravery has preceded you, Johanan. Gedaliah spoke highly of you."

"As he did of you," responded Johanan. "As does everyone."

156

"Courage comes in all clothing," he replied. "Mine was to merely wear truth in the midst of great confusion."

"A state of affairs that persists. Those who survived the treachery at Mizpah are camped not far from here. Others have joined us. We mean to leave shortly. Egypt seems the safest refuge. We would be honoured if you came with us."

"Yet you have not left. Instead you stand at Anathoth."

"Egypt is a great decision for us. But we would stay only until Nebuchadnezzar's anger is abated."

"Which would be when?" asked Jeremiah. "He is a young man. Ambitious. He has designs on Egypt."

"You see our dilemma clearly," Johanan said. "Whatever we do has risk. We need advice beyond ourselves in this matter. We need an oracle from Yahweh."

"Are you certain this is what you seek? Perhaps you seek a blessing for a journey you have already begun." Jeremiah's eyes twinkled. He was at ease and enjoying the exchange.

Baruch was less charitable. "Why come now and disturb my master's peace? If Egypt is your intention, then do what seems best to save yourselves. The oracles of Yahweh were not regarded in Jerusalem. Why would you heed them now?"

Johanan stiffened. "I was not in Jerusalem," he replied. "If the king would not listen to your advice, perhaps that is because some thought it came only from the pen of Baruch, not the mouth of his master."

"Enough," interjected Jeremiah. "Johanan was not in Jerusalem. You cannot vent your anger at him." Then, turning to look at Johanan, but continuing to address Baruch, he added, "However, Johanan and all the people he leads stand before us now and have not yet answered my question. Tell me, Johanan, do you really seek the mind of Yahweh in your decision? And even if he made it known to you, would you submit yourselves to it?"

"Petition your God on our behalf," replied Johanan, "and we who stand before you pledge by his own name that whatever is said will be obeyed. Whether it is for good or evil, we will obey the voice of Yahweh."[6]

"Have care, Johanan. Have care, all of you." Jeremiah's voice rose and deepened so that everyone could hear.

"It is no small thing to ask the mind of Yahweh. His thoughts are not just one more spice you toss into your deliberations and blend with the opinions of others. There are consequences even in the asking. The ignorant always fare better than the rebellious."

"What is the mind of Yahweh?" Johanan answered. "Are we to go to Egypt?" At the question, Jeremiah began to laugh.

"Do you think I carry around oracles in my bag like so much bread? Do you have any idea of the magnitude of your request?"

"I thought … I wasn't sure exactly how … I mean, I thought you might already know," Johanan finished. In truth, he had not the first idea how a prophet divined the mind of a god.

"You ask for more than you realize," said Jeremiah. There was sternness in his voice and sadness. "Since I was a youth, Yahweh's voice has been in my mouth. It is a burden I thought I could put down now in my old age. Yet for your sake, and because you have pledged to obey, I will do what you ask. Baruch will send for you when I have an answer." He rose heavily and Baruch helped him shuffle slowly out of the town square.

———

Doubt ambushed Johanan even before he reached home. There was no point in his staying at Geruth Chimham with Bethlehem so close. *What have I done? Every hour of delay increases our risk. Egypt is our only option, yet I have promised to wait on the oracle of some holy man whose God's temple lies in ruins.*

Inanna was making flat bread in large quantities when he returned. For some reason her actions infuriated him.

"Why are you baking so much bread?" he demanded.

"Because my husband said to make preparations for a journey," she replied icily. "Are we no longer going to Egypt?"

"I did not say that."

"Then we shall need as much food as we can carry." She did not stop nor was she about to press for information.

I told him not to go. Already trouble comes from it. It is all over his face.

He spoke into her stony silence. "Jeremiah has agreed to seek an oracle of instruction on our behalf and we will wait for it. Everyone has agreed to it."

"Everyone? I see."

"Yes, everyone. Those who were there, along with those who were not." *She is being obtuse and stubborn. Why do we always fight with the words left unsaid rather than with the words we use?*

"Am I to continue baking bread?"

"You may as well since you have started already."

"How long have we all agreed to wait?"

"I don't know. Jeremiah didn't say. These things aren't carried around in his purse, you know. Yahweh isn't pulled out from behind some kitchen jars and propped against a table leg for consultations."

"A day? A week? A month? Surely you must have some idea of how long we will wait.

"I didn't ask him. He promised us an oracle. We promised to wait."

But it was not a time for fighting. Neither of them wanted the isolation. They did not agree but had lived through too much chaos together to remain aloof for very long.

Finally, he spoke again in softer tones. "Continue in your preparations." A little of the helplessness that swirled inside of him leaked into his voice. And Inanna, who loved her husband dearly, caught his turmoil and held it with gentleness.

All around people continued to make ready for the flight to Egypt. Carts were repaired, extra sandals sewn and foodstuffs sorted. Everyone, it seemed, was seized by a need to keep busy and purposeful. Yet it was a dangerous pastime, difficult to reverse for many reasons.

Jeremiah sat inside his small house. Ever since the last time they had tried to kill him—when he'd been thrown into a cistern—he could find no position that was truly comfortable. He used pillows whenever he could. One shoulder was still out of joint from the ropes used to pull him out. Both knees had suffered badly from having stood for three days in the deep mud that was the floor of the cistern. And his beaten face was slow in healing.

Face the truth. You are old and should have died a long time ago. He did his best to hide his pain. Baruch's agitated hovering was often worse than the suffering. *Where is the dignity of old age? I cannot even be sovereign over my own discomforts.*

Just at that moment Baruch entered, carrying a cup he had overfilled with something hot. It was the third such beverage forced upon Jeremiah that day and it was not yet noon. "Warmed wine, sweetened with honey and herbs to ease your aches," said Baruch in a tone that made Jeremiah feel like an errant child.

He did not want the drink. He just wanted to be left alone. If he drank too much it only hastened a trip to the latrine, which, even though just outside in the yard, was an arduous journey.

"You are too kind," Jeremiah said. "Place it down near me and I'll drink it presently. He hoped the deflection would work. It usually didn't.

"It's better hot," Baruch replied. Baruch had joined himself to Jeremiah as scribe forty years earlier. Baruch's wife had left him long ago, and their only daughter, Shaheena, had been part of the first wave of hostages sent to live in Babylon. But Shaheena had died suddenly. Now all that was left of Baruch's family was his son-in-law Ezekiel and his only granddaughter named Sarah whom he had never seen. Both were still in Babylon. Jeremiah had never married, constrained by a word from Yahweh from doing so.

Jeremiah conceded and took the cup, putting it gingerly to his lips. Baruch continued to stand over him.

"Have you settled on what you will say to Johanan and the others? It's been three days now. They will be getting anxious."

"It is not yet clear in my mind."

"Ironic, isn't it?"

"What?"

"That our people end up everywhere but in our own land. It's sad enough that our best and most talented were deported to Babylon. Now it seems that even the few remaining dregs will go live in Egypt."

"That is not decided yet."

"But that is your first prescience is it not?"

"It would seem the most logical. It would not be the first time Yahweh hid his people in that land. You should not have chided Johanan the way you did, Baruch. He did not seek the leadership he carries. And he certainly cannot be held responsible for what happened in Jerusalem."

"True. But his own choice is still in front of him. What makes you think he is any more willing to listen to you than anyone else?"

"Nothing. However, since he has asked for advice, Yahweh will give it. Of that I am certain. It is his way."

Baruch sniffed. "Drink your wine before all the herbs settle to the bottom. I'll help you to the latrine later."

Jeremiah knew what to expect. It wasn't any more pleasant for being familiar. First would come all the people, floating like so much spring pollen in the limitless space of his imagination. He could see each one in detail, down to the stitching on their clothing and the wrinkles etched into their faces. Both those living and those who had died drifted together. The exiles in Babylon were as close as the rag-tag gathering that waited for him at Geruth Chimham. Kings he had served, court advisors, soldiers, some of whom had beaten him and some of whom had been his friends, market merchants and fellow prophets. It seemed to him that every Jew who had ever lived and who ever would live crowded into his mind. Time always collapsed under their numbers. There was no ordered sequence to their appearances. His father, long dead, would stand easily beside Baruch's granddaughter, who was by this time a sturdy child somewhere in Babylon. Josiah, the first king he'd served, would drift by in his chariot, Egyptian arrow still in his back. He wasn't dead, still upright and headstrong, bent on ridding the land of anything foreign. Right next to him would be the potter Jeremiah knew from the Jerusalem siege. He sat at his wheel shaping large wine jars. Jeremiah had been given an oracle once while standing in front of that potter. There was Pashur, the conniving chief priest who had locked him up in the stocks; there was his fellow prophet, Hananiah, still as fat as ever but now with a surprised look on his face—he'd been struck dead for having uttered oracles of his own devising.

Ever since Yahweh had claimed Jeremiah for special service—what was it, forty years earlier?—this pageant of all that ever was and would be had come to be the herald of Yahweh's voice. The people would gyrate around his mind, the scene so vast, so incomprehensible that he had long since given up trying to sort the players into chronological order. Future events wrapped through ancient history like jumbled vines. At first he thought himself a victim of an active imagination, visually storing and revisiting everything he'd seen and heard. Certainly as he grew older, the parade grew more complex, like a million glittering pieces of a mosaic whose ultimate pattern eluded him. It wasn't a question of standing too close to the image. They all existed in his mind, all at the same time. Each little tile—a person, a family, a coffin—could be seen in exquisite detail. Even the feelings of each figure would caress his own emotions, leaving a delicious vibration that resonated through his whole body. Brides on their wedding day full of hope, farmers gazing at ripe wheat, mothers laying out a dinner, children setting out with the goats in the early morning. The happy anticipation of these people illuminated the whole scene. His senses became a brilliantly played piece of music that continually built toward a crescendo that never arrived. Even the dark and tragic people, the cheaters, drunks and brutes, would pluck at some string and add a note that was both terrifying and enticing all at the same time.

Somewhere in the tightly packed maelstrom was Yahweh. His was the only tile that remained blurred and would not stop long enough for close examination. It was more like the silvery swirl of a fish's tail that broke the water for an instant before receding, only to surprise Jeremiah somewhere else. Nonetheless, Yahweh had put himself in the picture, existing as both artist and subject at the same time.

Such visions left Jeremiah restless and tense. It was Jeremiah's restlessness that distinguished the pageantry from idle daydreams, whose pace could be controlled and whose borders were secure. It was puzzling that such an infusion of images could be so disturbing and at the same time so magnificent. They left him quivering with energy so intense that he felt as if his whole body would fly apart into tiny pieces.

Slowly, over the years, he had come to understand the nature of his tension. It was not just his peoples' whole history that shimmered in front of him. Mixed in with what had been were also the histories that might have been. The decisions made differently or not made at all—every tiny decision made by each person created its own picture. But mixed together, in a way Jeremiah could never comprehend were the pictures of the same people taking different choices. It was a mosaic of infinite choices spanning infinite outcomes. No wonder there was never a resolution. The picture remained forever incomplete, pregnant with possibility. Josiah might show up just as easily without the arrow in his back; Hananiah and Jeremiah could have been friends. It was a potent mixture of both what was and what might have been.

This huge canvas was only the precursor to the more intimate manifestations of Yahweh. Out of all the scenes that were and might be, two would eventually crowd to the fore. These were the more detailed cameos, composed of the people of Jeremiah's age and to whom he spoke. Both scenes always contained the same people, each depicting the result of a pending choice. The scenes were rarely more than fragments of action, but enough for Jeremiah to divine how each outcome related to the decision at hand. These would be the scenes from which he would answer Johanan.

Few people had heeded Jeremiah during the forty years he'd been Yahweh's prophet. What made him weary was the weight of a stillborn history—permitted, even designed by Yahweh, yet rejected by the free will choices of his people. It was as if two painters fought over the same canvas and always Yahweh relinquished his palette.

What made him frantic was the spectre of a future that was often horrific but which did not have to be. This drove him to speak with a fierceness he did not naturally have, and it sparked the most dramatic of metaphors and public dramas so that no one would accuse him afterward of being shy and reticent. He did not mind the arrests. In a funny sort of way, he welcomed them as proof of his faithfulness. Was he gratified that he and he alone had declared the destruction of Jerusalem as proof of Yahweh's anger with his whoremongering people? No, in his darkest moments, he was guilt-ridden that there might have been something more he could have done to steer the people into different choices.

Forty years of failure. That was the legacy he would leave. And now Johanan stood before him. He was not a black-hearted miscreant who deserved to be expunged from the parade. Surely he merited a safe harbour, even within the obscurity of Egypt, to live out his days in quiet. It was not the life of choice, for already the choices of others had foreclosed on his own life. That was the tragedy of the larger mosaic; everyone's decisions were interdependent. Those with more power usually gouged the lives of those around them.

Surely the wrath of Yahweh had run its course. His city was laid waste, his temple obliterated and more than two-thirds of all Jews dead. If these few witless remnants sought to escape Nebuchadnezzar's indiscriminate reprisal for a crime Johanan himself had tried to prevent, where was the rebellion in that?

They came, as they inevitably came. Two futures. The first crept into his mind while he was half dozing in the sun outside his house. It started with himself. He was older, but looked in better health, as if he could walk unaided. Somewhere close at hand Baruch's happy, nagging voice was calling him to a meal. He was outside his same house here at Anathoth. They had not moved.

Johanan appeared, fatter now, wearing a plain tunic and the broad hat of a farmer. A young boy stood close to him, dressed much like his father. Little portraits of life from all over Judah appeared to Jeremiah, melted into a brilliant kaleidoscope of colour only to transmogrify into yet another scene. The roofs were back on houses, goats and sheep bleated in their enclosures, olive trees hung heavy with fruit. Even the ruins of Jerusalem looked more orderly. A small portico sheltering an altar now stood where the temple had been. The land was slowly healing. Yahweh had relented at last. He wanted them to stay.

The second future intruded swiftly, scattering the carefree happiness of the first collection. It showed scattered, unmarked graves in Egyptian soil. That was all. But it was enough.

By the seventh day he was certain of what entered his mind, sure that it was not of his own fabrication. It took another three days to find the words.

———

It was on the seventh night that Inanna had her dream. Ishtar visited her. Rarely did Inanna dream, and never had Ishtar been present.

The intensity of the experience stirred her enough so that part of her knew she was dreaming. *I am having a vision*, one part of her thought. *Whatever I do, I must not wake up. But I must remember.*

Ishtar was standing on a stone so that her already tall proportions allowed her to gaze out easily over a crowd that stood around her. She was looking directly at Inanna, singling her out from among the crowd and entering her every pore. She wore no clothing save a single amulet around her neck on which hung a small, shiny, six-pointed star. At the tip of each point what looked like a diamond caught the light and shot it out like white sparks. It was all the more striking against her copper skin—not the dull, common brown flesh tone. Ishtar's skin shone burnished bright as if a fiery heat lay just beneath it. It glistened, whether from oil or sweat Inanna could not tell. Her hair was coiled in braids and tied into a loose crown out of which ran two sheep's horns.

From somewhere a horse appeared and Ishtar leaped gracefully to its back. Her free hand now held a spear and as the image closed to where Inanna stood, she noticed a trickle of blood flowing from a small wound on Ishtar's thigh. The wound was not severe and the rivulet of rich red seemed more like jewelry. *She fights for us and is victorious.*

Horse and rider advanced until Ishtar's lean, sinewy leg was inches from Inanna's face. *If she touches me, I shall be consumed.* Gently the goddess leaned down until Innana felt Ishtar's breath on her face. The sheep's horns actually touched the top of Inanna's head and even through her sleep she felt the hard weight of the contact. *I am being anointed somehow. My devotion to her has not been in vain.*

The scenery around them changed again and Ishtar now stood on a dais that led up to the plinth of a delicately finished temple. She was framed between two carved pillars that supported a horizontal lintel that lofted upward into a sharp peak. Everything was covered with beaten gold and against it Ishtar's body took on even more brilliance. Her arms hung at her sides and she wore a robe that was diaphanous. It only served to heighten her nakedness and did not dim the six points of light that nestled in the groove of her breasts. *I am in Egypt*, Inanna's mind registered. *This is where I will make my offering of cakes and libation. This is my sanctuary.*

An intense hot contraction coursed through Inanna's whole body, not unlike her times with Johanan. She knew she was wet as she had never been before and she knew that Ishtar knew how keenly she had been aroused. *But this pleases Ishtar too. It is in the giving of pleasure that she too is satisfied.* It was the climax of a possession that had started with Ishtar's first glance and Inanna bathed in the intimate safety with abandonment.

Inanna woke to find that her dream had registered in all parts of her body and took the fact as proof of the vision's certainty. *Tokens from her realm so that I will know her presence is not false.* She felt deliriously light and free. Their path had at last been confirmed. There would be a new beginning for them all in Egypt.

She told Johanan over breakfast, which they ate outside in the early sun. He listened in silence. There was a vitality to her, a brightness that was new. He attributed it to the force of the experience itself, still only hours old. In time that would fade. But he also sensed a determination that was new and that worried him a great deal.

"I am glad you have been comforted in your sleep," he said finally. Not for him to raise the obvious issue.

"More than comfort. Guided. For me and the others. The heavens are not shut up to our distress and have given us a sign. Of that I am certain."

"Through you?"

"Do you think so little of me that you doubt it possible? Do not confuse your own ambivalence toward the things of Yahweh with my devotion to Ishtar. The truth, husband, is that all these years I have been more attentive to her than you have been to Yahweh. It is she who has heard my daily prayer for your safety." Inanna's tone was respectful.

Johanan could not challenge the facts. Despite his opposition she had been devout in her worship and strengthened as a consequence. He tried to think of the last time he had actually made a sacrifice to Yahweh or even offered prayers. It had to have been in Jerusalem. That would have been three, maybe four years back. *Yahweh's rituals prevent me from sneaking off into the ravines at every chance.* He did not voice a defence. The truth was that Ishtar was more present to Inanna than Yahweh had ever been to him. And for that he was envious.

He chose a more reasoned response. "Jeremiah has spent his whole life grasping the thoughts of Yahweh. It is his vocation, like fighting and farming are mine. Our way is to leave these matters to those who are trained in them. You have the experience of a night."

"But we have had no need for Ishtar's counsel until now— only her protection for those who sought it. And there are many among us who worship as I do.

It was true. The reality was that there were as many deities worshipped throughout the land as there were towns. That had always been the most contentious issue among the Yahweh prophets. "No gods save Yahweh" was the first and supreme rule. But not many people adhered to it. Johanan knew that in certain quarters Inanna's vision would be received with celebration and relief. *And who am I to challenge another's beliefs? Yahweh has never shown himself to me. Have I not fought his enemies these past three years? And what has been the result?*

"It will go well for us when Jeremiah confirms your insight," he said. "Two gods watching over us is a good omen."

"And should his words be different? What then?"

"I need to walk."

"And I am going to share my oracle with others who are in sympathy with me. There is nothing more that needs doing. We could leave for Egypt any time. This is a day of glad tidings."

From dream to oracle in less than an hour. She will not relinquish this experience readily.

Johanan did not know how to even think cogently about his wife's vision or its implication. There was a tightness in his bowels that he recognized as the panic of indecision. *Suppose Jeremiah's allocution opposes my wife's dream? I know nothing of this man or his motives. Who knows what really went on inside Jerusalem? Some think he was in the pay of Nebuchadnezzar. Inanna would never play me false. All these years she has been my helpmate. I could not have asked for anyone more loyal. She credits our safety to the watchful eye of Ishtar. I do not know this Ishtar, but is she any less real than Yahweh? She is real enough to Inanna, more than Yahweh is to me. Whatever else, she has told me the truth as she knows it. Why did I go to Jeremiah in the first place? The logic of Egypt is unequivocal. We cannot stay and expect peace. Gedaliah trusted in Yahweh's protection and it did him no good.*

Round and round in his head marched the questions like dancers looking for partners that could not be found.

———

How much Inanna's dream influenced others, Johanan could not judge. For sure it was common knowledge among those who had prepared to leave. By the tenth day, the prevailing mood was to depart. And that was the day Baruch arrived saying that Jeremiah had an answer for them.

The small town square of Anathoth was packed with people eager to hear the news. Jeremiah stood this time, leaning heavily into his stick.

"You sent for us," said Johanan without preamble. "What news?"

"Yahweh has been gracious and revealed his mind."

Spare me the prologue, thought Johanan. *Just tell us.* But he replied with equal solemnity. "What says Yahweh?"

"That you should remain in this land. Nebuchadnezzar will not harm you. Stay in your homes, plant and harvest. Worship Yahweh in quietness and it will go well with you and your children. Yahweh's anger is finished. He weeps over those who have died and sits as one in mourning for his children.[7] To you he will be merciful."

Jeremiah's voice became less formal and more animated. He stared fixedly into every face that would meet his eye. "All of you, listen carefully to this news. Yahweh has blessed me at last with an oracle of glad tidings for his people. He has repented of his vengeance and will build you up, not destroy you as he has so many. Listen to my words. They are not burdensome. Only remain in the land."

He had begun to move as best he could, caught up in the ebullience of his own words. It was the voice of someone pleading against enormous skepticism. Even before they had gathered, the momentum was toward Egypt, and Jeremiah saw that it remained tilted heavily in that direction. He could see it in their faces. He spoke again, saying the same message with more force, with greater optimism, trying to bend his bruised face so that it would deliver the compassion that he was certain Yahweh now held for this tiny group of leftover people.

But it did no good. *One more failure.*

Johanan sensed an irritation in the crowd, as if accosted by a persistent beggar who only slowed them down. He knew at once that Jeremiah's advice would be ignored. *All we needed was a departing blessing and even that you withhold. Why do you sting us with words you know we cannot follow? Do you hate us that much? Besides, I am not a king. I cannot command these people to stay.*

"These words, this oracle you utter in the name of Yahweh, surely it is the fabrication of your longing for better times—for life as it was," Johanan said. "But it cannot be true, for there is safety only in Egypt, we both know that."

"Do you accuse my master of speaking falsely?" interjected Baruch. His beard tip quivered like an angry tentacle.

"I say his words are false, not the man."

"I do not see a difference."

"Perhaps the words are not Jeremiah's."

"What do you imply. Whose words would they be?"

"Yours, of course. You seem to have a great need to see us all destroyed by the Babylonians. Who is to say that the venom you have stored within you has not seized Jeremiah?"

"Why? To what end?" Baruch's voice was shrill and his bald head glowed pink. It only made him an easier foil.

"Because you seek the approval of Nebuchadnezzar. It would make an ingratiating tale to tell him, how you deceived us into staying here by inventing a false oracle in the name of Yahweh—and then encouraging it in the feeble mind of your master."

"Liar!" Baruch raged. "Your hearts are as depraved as those who abused us in Jerusalem. Go to Egypt then. Go there and die like the heathen jackals you are."

"We should have departed ten days ago. And it is what we will do now."

Jeremiah spoke again. "Johanan, all of you. It was you who sought these words. I did not press them on you. And you yourselves pledged by everything sacred to abide by the outcome. It is true. You could have left these ten days past. And I—I would have blessed your journey willingly."

"But you will not do that now? Why?"

"Because you sought Yahweh and he has answered you. It is not my fault that his words are not to your liking."

"And so you have no benediction as we depart?"

"Only the benediction of Yahweh."

"And what would that be?"

"That if you leave, you go astray at the cost of your own lives. You shall never return. Neither will your children, for they will perish with you in Egypt. Just as I destroyed all those in Jerusalem who did not obey me, so will I destroy you. Now therefore know for a certainty that you shall die by the sword, by famine and by pestilence in the place where you desire to go. Egypt will be your grave. Thus says Yahweh."

"Then it will be yours as well," replied Johanan with a brazenness he did not feel. "We will not leave you here to betray us to the Babylonians when they come. Pack your belongings. You and Baruch are coming with us."

Epilogue

Jeremiah traveled to Egypt with the fugitives. He continued to preach against idolatry. But "all the men who knew that their wives had offered incense to other gods and all the women ... said: 'We will continue to burn incense to the Queen of Heaven as we did in the cities of Judah; for then we had plenty. But since we left off burning incense and pouring out libations to her we have lacked everything and have been consumed by the sword and by famine.' And the women said, 'Was it without our husbands' approval that we made cakes for her bearing her image?'"[8]

Jeremiah promised their destruction—that they would become an execration, a horror, a curse and a taunt. In order that they would know the truth of his prophecy, he predicted that the Pharaoh Hophra would fall into the hands of his enemies, just as Zedekiah had fallen to Nebuchadnezzar. Hophra was executed in the aftermath of a civil war in 570 BC. It is not known whether Jeremiah lived to see his oracle's fulfilment.

Endnotes

[1] While the "wives of Judah" are referred to as a group, no individual is named. This character is the only fictitious person inserted into the story. All other names and lineages are historical. The name "Inanna" translates literally to "Lady of Heaven" and is the Summerian rendering for "Ishtar," the Mesopotamian goddess of love and war.

[2] Nebuzaradan, the "captain of the guard," took charge of the final stages of the Jerusalem campaign. He deported a large number of Jews who had survived within the city, burned the major buildings and broke down the city walls. He was also given responsibility to ensure the safety of Jeremiah and invited him to return to Babylon as an honoured advisor. Jeremiah declined, choosing instead to remain with the poor people of the land who owned nothing. Jeremiah 39:9 and elsewhere in the chapter.

[3] For the complete story of Jeremiah's land purchase, see Jeremiah 32:6-15

[4] Jeremiah 40:12

[5] Jeremiah 40:15 speaks of a secret meeting between the two men. Johanan's primary concern is the welfare of the remnant and he argues again that Gedaliah's death would be catastrophic.

[6] Jeremiah 42:6.

[7] Jeremiah 42:10, in the Revised Standard Version, reads "... for I repent of the evil which I did to you." Some scholars argue that this is an inadequate translation for the Hebrew verb, the sense of which is "to take a deep breath" (sigh sorrowfully).

[8] Excerpts from Jeremiah 44ff.

BABYLON POST

To Ezekiel, a priest to the exiles at Babylon, from Baruch, living at Tahpanhes in Egypt:

I write to you finally, after such a long silence with terrible news. Jeremiah is dead. I did not know who else to write. Certainly, there is no one living near the ruins of Jerusalem who would know his name, much less mourn. You, and you alone are the last true servant of Yahweh and if this letter reaches you, I know you will put ashes on your head, cover your face and sit in sadness for the prescribed days.

He did not suffer long toward the end. It was clear even as we left Judah that he was frail. He had suffered much when confined in Jerusalem—before it fell—and never did revive fully. He got back some strength these past five years we have lived in Egypt. And his intimacy with Yahweh remained vibrant for he declared many oracles and yes, even a public drama.[1] It reminded me of his old self when he did such things in Jerusalem. This past half year he weakened quickly and could not move about anywhere without my helping him. This I did gladly. But finally he could not even leave his bed and refused much of his food. In the end he fell into a kind of deep sleep and never wakened.

I wish I could tell you that his burial here in Egypt was full of honour and respect. It was not. It was more as if people preferred to believe he had never lived, and that they had not forced him to journey with them when we fled, after Gedaliah was murdered. Five men—five men only—came and helped me bury him and have sat with me these past days. Johanan was one of them, much to my

surprise. I did not like him any the more for it. If he feels
remorse in leading us down here, he keeps it within himself. I have built up a cairn as best I can over Jeremiah's
grave. It sits apart in the patch of land we use as our cem-
etery. But we die all too quickly and I am sure he will be
encroached on soon enough.

Such a shabby end. Down to Egypt we came, certainly against my will. He was their talisman against the anger
of Yahweh, and yet even this insult he ignored. My only
solace is that his predictions about what would happen to
them is fulfilled in our midst. Everyone knows it, though
few admit it. Hostile neighbours and harsh soil is our
lot down here. I do not think our settlement will survive
beyond the people who first arrived. And, scandal that it
is, my heart rejoices that these people will die.

They have given themselves entirely over to the worship of Ishtar. A few of the imaginative ones speak of
Ishtar as the consort to Yahweh, and in this way delude
themselves into thinking that the Ishtar rituals are at
least not in opposition to the things of Yahweh. Inanna,
Johanan's wife, has become an acolyte within the Ishtar
order of priestesses. She gives herself freely over to the
fertility rites ....

Baruch paused to read over what he had written thus far. His
escritoire was outside, pushed up against the back wall of his hut. From
noon onward, the sunlight was clear and unfettered. The location meant
he endured the vagaries of the wind blowing up the edges of his papyri
and depositing layers of fine dust in the still-wet ink. But his eyes could
no longer tolerate the gloom that lay within. He accepted his limitations
with the stoicism of a professional, aging scribe who had written in
much worse surroundings.

I sound angry and distraught, he thought, reading back over his
page. *Ezekiel will think me old and labile, pouring out my heart after
such a long silence. And to suggest that Inanna is a temple whore, why
should Ezekiel care? He does not even know her. Yet I still blame her
for her part in bringing us here—her and her husband, Johanan. Five
years later and I am still angry. Well, he is my son-in-law—that should
count for something. And age has its privileges. He will have to read it.*

176

Seventeen years earlier,[2] Baruch's only daughter, Shaheena, had married Ezekiel. They were in the first wave of deportees to Babylon—all young and talented people. Not until Ezekiel reached Babylon did Yahweh's spirit fall heavily on him. Some would say too heavily, for his prophetic behaviour was eccentric in the extreme. Despite his frequently audacious antics, no one argued that he wasn't the genuine article. For that he was respected. However, Ezekiel's vocation had put a heavy strain on Shaheena. They had one daughter. Her name was Sarah.

Shaheena had died in Babylon, under tragic and clouded circumstances. Ezekiel, though not culpable, had been involved. Somehow, her death had been manipulated into some grotesque kind of prophetic object lesson. The incident surpassed bad taste. Ezekiel's deportment had bordered on the ghoulish. Baruch had separated from his own wife long ago and had loved Shaheena with all the muddied passion of a man who is already lonely. Relations between the father and son-in-law remained awkward. *But it goes beyond my daughter,* he thought. *Ezekiel's oracles were always so fantastical and extreme. He is not as disciplined as Jeremiah is ... was.*

Baruch picked up his stylus once more to write. *What else is there to tell him? Jeremiah is dead. The only proofs that he ever lived are a mound of stones and a clay jar stuffed full of manuscripts—his oracles and that no one ever heeded. My life, too, resides inside that jar. I had such hopes for myself when I first joined Jeremiah, hopes for everyone. His oracles were such powerful insights and I polished them until they dazzled. They could have saved us all.*

He sighed and continued his letter.

> You should know that I still possess in written form the bulk of Jeremiah's oracles. Ever since King Jehoiakim[3] burned my first scroll as a drunken palace amusement, I have been careful to guard my writings and have committed long portions to memory. As a memorial to my master, I have pledged myself to create a full collection of his oracles. My plan is to include accounts of his more impressive dramatizations. There is much work required, but I have no other tasks. The one good thing about Egypt is the abundance of quality papyri. The rumours that they

sell only the second rate sheets to the caravans is true. The scribe in me is glad.

I fear, however, for the rough transmissions I have already at hand. There is no one among us here that would save them. Should harm befall me, that would be the end. The finished work, if Yahweh permits me life enough to complete it, should rest in your care. There is no one else. How to see it safely to Babylon is still a problem. For the moment, I find solace in arranging my material. Already I have gathered all the oracles of judgements that Jeremiah pronounced on the ten nations.[4] You will take heart to know that Babylon is among the nations whom Yahweh will punish sorely. I will send you a copy of that particular one when I am able.

Write me with the news of Sarah. She is all that I have left of my family, and you as well.

BY MY OWN HAND, BARUCH.

He debated about trying to change his closing salutation; the inclusion of Ezekiel as family was an obvious afterthought. *Perhaps in the morning, if I have energy, I will rewrite the last page. Certainly I will not cross it out and show that I have made a mistake.*

But in the morning, he did not rewrite the letter. Once a thing was written, it was hard for him to change it. Scribes were above making mistakes. It would also have meant making the change twice for he always took the precaution of sending a second copy by way of a different courier. Most people did not since it meant more expense both in the sending and in the manumission. But since Baruch wrote his own letters, it was only the cost of the extra courier he had to think about.

Tahpanhes was a well-developed outpost on the eastern edge of the Nile's delta. A fortified garrison and several elaborate temples gave it substance. The Ishtar temple, in particular, was magnificent, and the Jewish refugees were welcomed as adherents into the active cult that operated in the area. Tahpanhes's markets were brisk. For Baruch's needs, its chief advantage was that it lay on the established caravan route. The Jewish immigrants lived in a kind of shantytown that lay a good distance from the town's centre. It took Baruch almost an hour to make his way to the market centre and begin his search for couriers.

One copy of the letter would go by way of the traditional trading route—north, about 600 miles, roughly parallel to the Great Sea, then east, another 500 miles, to Babylon. The route followed a path that looked something like a giant, curved harvesting scythe. Egypt and Babylon were its two ends and all that lay between was known as the Fertile Crescent. The speed with which a letter might travel the distance depended entirely on the whims of the caravaner who carried it.

There was a second, faster route to Babylon, but it meant crossing directly across the Arabian desert and was accomplished only by fast, mounted riders who specialized in the journey. Attrition rates were high on this 700-mile "express" route; the hazards of geography and hostile nomads commanded a higher price.

Baruch did not really need the security of two couriers. The consequence of this letter's being lost was slight. Nothing in it was particularly urgent. But it would be up to four months before a reply might be even reasonably expected, and if none came it meant starting the whole process over again. That he decided to contract with a courier that would travel the faster route only confirmed his need to connect. Yet if he had been challenged on the subject he would only have scoffed and made a caustic reply about the perils of imprudence.

Returning to his hut, his first act was to check his jar. It was made in the manner of a wine jug, three feet tall and over a foot in diameter. Years ago in Jerusalem, he had commissioned it for just this purpose. The neck was narrower than the body and a fitted clay lid fit neatly into its recessed rim. Baruch had carefully applied a ring of soft pitch around the edge of the lid that sealed when he pushed it down onto the neck of the urn. This permitted the jug to lie on its side without the lid falling off. The last embellishment Baruch had added was a thin layer of braided straw glued in tight coils to the outside, which had kept the jar from breaking on more than one occasion. The jar had suffered much over the years. Once, during the height of King Jehoiakim's anger with Jeremiah and himself, he had hidden it suspended from ropes inside a well.

Baruch hid his urn in a trench he had dug in the floor of his hut. He kept a thin layer of loose dirt on top, which, in turn, was covered by his sleeping pallet. He was always anxious when separated from the urn and would check on its safety several times each day. When they had first arrived, whenever he entered his hut after an absence, he always scraped away the loose earth, loosened the lid and put his hand inside until he could touch the bundles of papyri and vellum. On entering his hut now, however, he only scraped away enough dirt to see that the jar still lay beneath.

His life was easier than that of most of the refugees who had come down to Egypt. He still had some money and worked readily enough as a scribe whenever asked. He could have opened a stall in the market to ply his trade. It would have meant more language study—the Egyptians had abandoned their hieroglyphics in favour of a simpler hieratic script—but their new alphabet wasn't difficult for him. But he lacked the ear for the spoken word and so dictation would have been a problem. His needs were modest and enough people knew him that he could rely on the customers who sought him out. They were fellow Jews, for the main part, and Baruch tolerated them for the sake of social contact.

I have even made a truce with Johanan, he thought. *Now that is proof that I am lonelier than I realize.* Johanan was the de facto leader among the Jews. Formerly a guerrilla resistance fighter against Nebuchadnezzar, he had been responsible for bringing Jeremiah and Baruch to Egypt. And just now, it was his voice calling to Baruch from without.

"I'm coming," answered Baruch, making sure that his jar was properly lodged. "What do you want?" he asked, emerging from his hut.

"You've come from the market?"

"I've sent letters to Babylon—to Jews who still follow Yahweh."

Johanan ignored the insult. Their barbed exchanges were like dogs who ritually peed on each other's boundary markets. But they were careful to keep their differences contained.

"Did you hear any news of the war?"

"Nothing new. The traders I spoke to are heading north, out of Egypt. No one trades in the west these days. The campaign against Libya does not go well for Pharaoh Hophra. The region is much too unsettled for trade."

Johanan pressed his lips together. Baruch observed him critically. *He is still making up his mind whether to share his news with me.* But the rift between the two men wasn't personal and at present they were both Jewish refugees perched precariously in a foreign land.

"I've come from the garrison," Johanan said. "The rumour is that the Egyptians have been badly beaten."

"What of it?"

"The troops blame Hophra, who did not go with them but remained in Memphis. They say the whole conflict was ill conceived and unnecessary. And the army has refused to engage the Libyans again."

"So, they will march back to Memphis and lick their wounds," replied Baruch. "None of this concerns us."

"The armies are not marching back. They have established Saqqara as headquarters and have sent demands that Hophra relinquish the throne. He is arrogant and incompetent, so they say."

Baruch snorted. "What king isn't? Still, what they have done is an act of treason."

"If the field army was small, and comprised of provisionals, I would agree. But they are neither. They form about half of the professional corps and some of their officers survived the carnage at Carchemish. No, this is not treason. It is a civil war."

Baruch's bowels tightened involuntarily at the words. *Is there no peace anywhere in the world?* Aloud he said, "What will happen?"

"Hophra has sent a General Amasis, his chief of command, to put down the revolt. He has already left Memphis with troops. Some of the garrison here at Tahpanhes were seconded to the mission."

"Do you mean to tell me that Egypt marches against Egypt?"

"I do. I had hoped you would have more news from the merchants."

"I'm sorry, but I will be diligent in my enquiries. This is not good news for us. We will be pressed to take sides. Everyone will. Yet, it is hardly our conflict. For the moment we are safe. We are a hundred miles from Memphis, and Saqqara is one hundred miles further west than that."

The two men looked at each other as if to say, "if both of us say aloud that we are safe, perhaps we can convince ourselves it is so."

Baruch returned to his work. Most of his days were spent at his table, pushed against the back wall of his hut, reading and arranging the contents of his urn. Each sheaf of papyri he touched was like an old friend. He could remember clearly all the details of its creation. Holding one in his hand, he could move easily into its own time and place. They were like little pictures of his life, laid out according to age. His practised eye saw all the stages of his vocation. They were not all neat. Some had been written quickly and in bad light. His writing had grown smaller over time, forced on him first when papyri had been scarce and expensive. It had meant that he cut his reed styli even thinner than usual. They did not last as long but cost next to nothing. The inks had changed over the years, depending on what was available. The basic recipe was always charcoal mixed with finely ground slag obtained from a metal smith. He bought them in small, round cakes. To actually make a mark meant first wetting the reed stylus and then working it around the cake's surface until a black syrupy liquid formed. Like everything else, the quality of inks varied greatly.

Jeremiah referred to my stylus once, thought Baruch fondly.

"The sin of Judah is written with a pen of iron; with a point of diamond it is engraved on the tablet of their heart." He knew the words by heart.[5] He always delighted whenever Jeremiah would utter some allusion to Baruch's involvement, or to his craft. Baruch had never attempted to inscribe stone. It was a different craft. *But my words cut just as deeply ... his words. Without scribes, the whole world lasts only a single generation. It is we who are the keepers of memory and custodians of knowledge.*

The days turned to weeks and then to months. Baruch revelled deeper in his retrospections. When a man's life ends before he has died, there is only the past to occupy him. Until one day, a letter arrived back from Babylon.

FROM EZEKIEL THE SON OF BUZI, AT BABYLON, TO BARUCH, THE SCRIBE AMONG THE EXILES AT TAHPANHES:

Father. May I not give offence by the word, but in truth that is the word uppermost in my mind as I write. Sorrow upon sorrows that I could not be with you at Jeremiah's death. You loved him as no other person did. Even now, I picture you guarding his memory, serving him long past the appointed term. I console you with news that when your letter arrived, many of us here mourned. Here at least he is honoured, for his words first gave us hope. You must remember his letter to us, for you wrote it, I am sure.

"Stay in the land and seek the welfare of Babylon. Build houses and plant gardens. Take wives, have children and give your daughters in marriage. For when seventy years are completed Yahweh will bring you back and give you a future and a hope."

We did not accord it much attention at first. Not until Jerusalem was destroyed. Now we wait, and it was Jeremiah who gave us the assurances that we have not been abandoned. I know in Jerusalem he was not seen in that light, but here in Babylon we have only his one oracle of encouragement—not counting the one that was thrown in the river. Surely a copy of that one remains among your notes.

We are like our ancestors who followed Moses out into the desert only to discover that their children would enter the Promised Land —not themselves. Yet, I sense no rancour among us. We had already lived a decade away from temple and city before Jerusalem was destroyed. I feel more for those among you who carry the carnage forever in your minds. In our minds, Jerusalem is the way we left it.

I have not followed Jeremiah's whole advice for I remain unmarried. Sarah grows each day. She stays with me, but receives tender care from others ....

Tears blurred the letter so that Baruch had to stop reading. *He lives my own life over again.* He felt instantly all the guilty love that only a single parent knows. *To raise a son without a wife; that could be done without much harm. But a daughter.* There were vast parts of life he had never prepared Shaheena for, simply because he did not know them himself. Often he had thought of remarrying only for Shaheena's sake. *But I failed once in that endeavour. A second time might have been worse. I was not an easy man to please.* He wiped his eyes and continued to read.

I do not think I harm the child by remaining unwed. You are the only man alive who will understand when

I say that Shaheena still lives on in my head and in my heart. I have only to look at Sarah to be reminded. Sarah remains the object of my love, however poorly I render it to action. Somehow in loving her, I get to love Shaheena in all the ways I was prevented. There is a peace about it.

But I have come to realize better the agony you must have felt when Shaheena died. And my own apparent indifference must have been great bitterness in your mouth. I have only to imagine the same thing befalling Sarah and instantly I am stricken with a tiny portion of your despair. Forgive me, Father. Even after all these years I still wonder if there was something I could have done to change the mind of Yahweh.

Your ambition to compile the oracles of Jeremiah is laudable beyond words. Would that I had someone half as competent here at my side. There are a few scribes who attend me and they mean well enough. But your eye does not overlook a single detail, and you do not lose sight of the truth. Send me what you can when you are ready. Perhaps in sections would be the safest.

I do not make this last observation lightly. You should know that Hophra's difficulties are being closely followed at the Babylonian court. The widespread belief is that Nebuchadnezzar will take advantage of the situation and march against Egypt. He has not campaigned that way since Jerusalem fell and he has yet to put his foot on Egyptian soil. The mud of Egypt on his sandals is a trophy he dearly covets. Be prudent in your affairs. I will send you more news as I am able.

EZEKIEL, BY MY OWN HAND.

It was a magnificent letter to get, beyond what Baruch had expected. *Or my letter deserved*, he thought. He devoured the letter in the ensuing weeks, sucking every nuance from it as he would the small bits of meat hidden inside the legs of a river crab. *So at least one of Jeremiah's visions was not in vain. But it is always the pleasant pronouncements that people remember and honour—never the warnings.*

Baruch did indeed remember the scroll that was now nothing but river mud somewhere in the Euphrates. He'd written it ten years before the fall. King Zedekiah was the vassal of Nebuchadnezzar and was four years into his thirteen long years of ineptitude. The tribute required by Babylon was steep and Zedekiah resented being little more than a tax collector. There were four other sovereigns, neighbours to Judah who were also feeling the pecuniary pricks of their common master. Clandestine consultations were held, and Zedekiah had been unlucky enough to have hosted a meeting at Jerusalem.

Nebuchadnezzar was informed. Within a five-nation conspiracy, it was impossible for there not to be a spy somewhere. Fortunately for the conspirators, Nebuchadnezzar's armies were occupied elsewhere and all that happened was that Zedekiah was summoned to Babylon to explain himself.[6]

Jeremiah, convicted by Yahweh that Babylon herself would be overrun, had composed a number of poetic judgements prophesying her savage demise. When he heard that a court delegation was going to Babylon, he saw his chance.

"Baruch," he had said, "the oracles against Babylon; they must be proclaimed within her borders."

"Zedekiah goes to grovel not to growl," Baruch had replied. "I do not think Nebuchadnezzar would be amused at your dirge. They leave no room for doubt."

"No, I agree. But still I feel it is essential that these words of mine—words of Yahweh—live in the land they are meant for."

"Does it add to their powers?" Baruch had asked.

"In truth, I am not sure. But I think so. What good are my oracles if they are hidden? What good is any prophecy if the people cannot hear the thoughts of Yahweh, and perhaps repent? Besides, I believe this is an imperative of Yahweh."

"Why not just read them here? Surely they would be well received."

"Too well received, I am afraid. They would be taken as false hope. There are enough prophets who utter soothing pap about Nebuchadnezzar's quick dispatch. I have no wish to mix my words with theirs."

"But if it is the same message, what is the difference?"

"The difference is that Babylon will fall only after it has been the instrument of our own destruction. Until then, it pleases Yahweh to strengthen her. All nations serve Yahweh, whether they know it or not."

"But how do you propose to have your oracles read? And the scroll you want me to prepare—whoever has it—it would be like clutching a scorpion to his bosom. He would be killed if it were discovered."

Jeremiah's eyes had shone with the excitement of a child who has discovered how to outwit his parents. "Your brother might do it for us, if you asked him."

Baruch gasped at Jeremiah's temerity. "You want Seraiah to carry your scroll and then read it aloud in Babylon? He is Zedekiah's quartermaster, not even a civilian. If he's caught, he will die a particularly cruel death."

"But if you asked him, he might be persuaded to do it as a favour."

Baruch arranged for them to meet with his brother.

"You want me to do what?" asked Seraiah when he met them. "You are both crazed."

"It is the wish of Yahweh," Jeremiah said imperiously. But the grin on his face was a frank invitation to join in a wonderful adventure. Seraiah looked rapidly back and forth between their faces, assessing whether he was the object of a prank.

"Is this some kind of distorted jape?" he asked.

"Only on the Babylonians, I assure you," replied Jeremiah.

"How long is the scroll? How many oracles? You are not known for brevity, Jeremiah. And are you certain Yahweh commands it?"

Baruch had known at that moment that his brother would do it for them. He warmed in the vicarious glow of performing a special service to Jeremiah.

"I do not have to send all that Baruch has written down. He will make a special copy of selected portions."

"And afterwards?" Seraiah asked. "After I complete the most insane thing I will have ever done? I do not wish to keep the document on my personage. There are enough risks just carrying it on the journey to Babylon. I know of no one among the exiles to leave it with. No one that I trust with the knowledge that I smuggled it into Babylon."

Jeremiah was waiting for the question. It was the apex of the adventure. "Afterwards? Why afterwards you must tie a large stone to the scroll and hurl it far out into the Euphrates. And after you have done that, you must say the words, 'thus shall Babylon sink to rise no more, because of the evil that I, Yahweh, am bringing upon her.'"[7]

Seraiah turned to Baruch, his face awash with incredulity. "This request, this melodrama that risks my life—does it make *any* sense to you?"

"Pick a quiet moment. Slip away and read the words while standing on the riverbank and then toss it in," Baruch replied, not answering the question. "You cannot draw your sword against our overlords, so why not your tongue? Besides, it will make a great tale to tell afterwards to your grandchildren. Zedekiah slobbering all over the signet ring of Nebuchadnezzar, and you uttering imprecations on a riverbank, all in the same trip."

"Must I have an audience?" Seraiah had asked.

"Seek out Ezekiel if you can," Jeremiah answered. "He will understand the import of what you do."

Seraiah had done what he was asked, convinced that if his brother wasn't mad, his employer certainly was. But that was years ago, when everyone had been young and reckless.

Seraiah did not live to tell the tale to his children, much less grandchildren. He was faithful to Zedekiah right up to the end and was executed along with all his other officers and city officials.[8] *The gratitude of Yahweh is a mystery*, thought Baruch as he sifted through the papyri looking for the draft of the scroll he had written out. *But I shall include my brother's name and what he did somewhere in my account of Jeremiah's words. That is the least I can do for you, dear brother.*

He missed his brother at that moment—it was a hot longing that pierced the scales of stoicism that he had grown to fend off disappointment. *I am too old to miss him*, he thought. *Yet here I sit blubbering like a hired mourner as if his death was yesterday. What should it matter now, after everyone has gone? He was not the only good man to die. Zephaniah was executed along with him—I must find a place to mention him as well.[9] And others must be included so that whoever reads my work will know that we were not all depraved lechers no longer fit to occupy the same universe as Yahweh. Some stayed true. I would not be alive if they had not helped.*

The act of cataloguing worthy people whose deeds of courage needed inclusion somewhere within Jeremiah's oracles carried Baruch safely out of his grief back to the task he had chosen for the day. It escaped his notice that he might have been crying out of guilt that he was still alive.

He was nervous about dying. It was not an emotional phobia, but simply a practical eventuality that had to be considered and planned around—one more detail in the fastidious labyrinth that was Baruch's mind, which demanded the making of contingencies. *Jeremiah would never forgive me if I died with his oracles in such chaos.* The absurd convolutions of his mind made even him smile. *I will start by making copies of sections that are already complete. And I will start with the most important ones. Ezekiel must acknowledge the receipt of each section so that if I should die suddenly, everything will not perish with me. But first, I must speak with Johanan. Ezekiel's news will not be welcome.* Baruch smiled at the thought of being the herald of bad news. *Serves him right.*

"How long do you think the letter took to come from Babylon?" Johanan asked. He was an impoverished refugee, but no less able to assess military intelligence.

"Six months perhaps. The merchant who delivered it was not from Babylon. He accepted it from his trading partner who travels only as far as Carchemish. I'm not really sure."

"You have heard of General Amasis's exploits?"

"The Commander-in-chief sent by the Pharaoh to put down the revolt? What of him?"

"He is now crowned a king and has established a government at Saqqara. Two-thirds of the army support him. Pharaoh Hophra is virtually a prisoner within Memphis. He cannot leave the city and hasn't the troops to attack. However, the troops who follow him are dedicated. General Amasis is avoiding a final confrontation. He waits and diverts taxes to his coffers, weakening Hophra by doing so. For the moment, it is a stalemate. But it cannot stay that way forever. Either the country will be partitioned or one of the kings will be killed."

"Or," Baruch replied, "if Ezekiel's news is reliable, Nebuchadnezzar will come and conquer them both."

"It never ends, does it?" answered Johanan.

Baruch choked down the obvious retort. *It would have, if we'd stayed in our homeland, as Jeremiah advised.* There was no point in debating what might have been. Instead he said, "Johanan, were you present at Jeremiah's last public drama?"

"No, but I heard of it. You want me to believe that Nebuchadnezzar will come and walk upon the bricks that Jeremiah buried?"

"That was the oracle."

"Baruch, Jeremiah is dead and with him died his words."

That is not true, and you know it. But you can never admit it, not while your wife still leads you around by your testicles. However, he only answered , "So you hope."

"What's to be done?"

"Nothing. We wait."

Baruch set about making a copy of his most prized text. *The Fire Scroll* he called it. He loved the irony of its name and even touching it brought back all the hot urgency that he felt when he had first written it—back in days of King Jehoiakim, who was thought to be the worst king of Judah until Zedekiah succeeded him and established a new low. In fact, *The Fire Scroll* was a copy of an earlier text that King Jehoiakim had burned, just before ordering the arrest of Jeremiah and Baruch. They had hidden for six months in a concealed cellar, under the flooring of an old warehouse owned by Baruch's father. Only Baruch's father and one trusted family servant knew their whereabouts and kept them supplied.[10] The remaking of the scroll had been Baruch's salvation. The cellar was only fifteen feet square and without something to occupy his time Baruch would have gone mad.

The copy he was now making for Ezekiel was on vellum. Baruch had debated the decision for a long time. There was a tradition among the Jews that the law books of Moses were always copied on leather hides. Baruch, never one to pass on a chance to enhance the status of his work, wanted Jeremiah's oracles treated with equal reverence. But it was not simply a matter of choosing between two differing qualities of the same medium. Vellum required different pens and inks from papyrus. The inks contained tree resin and dried slowly, and the ink never stuck to the parchment in quite the same way as it soaked into papyrus. Errors in a parchment document could be scraped off with a sharp knife and even whole scrolls could be erased by a vigorous wash in a mixture of water and lime. Their presentation was, however, majestic. The really goods ones were works of art. Touching them was a richly sensual experience.

In the end, presentation won out over other considerations. He bought a length of virgin skin, creamy white and stitched together with a matching thread. He would be careful not to make any errors and hope that over time, the ink would adhere. His usual second copy would be on papyrus and sent ahead as a herald of the authentic item.

It took over three months. Baruch worked only in the direct sunlight of the afternoon sun and rendered a scroll that was a work of art. *Now for a letter that explains it,* he thought.

> To Ezekiel, a priest at Babylon among the exiles, from Baruch, the scribe of Jeremiah, at Tahpanhes in Egypt
>
> My Son, Thanks be to Yahweh for the safety of you and Sarah. May his care continue. Here is it well with me. Your letter was like a cold drink offered in the heat of noon. I keep it close to me and in that way keep you and Sarah close as well.

He stared at his opening salutation fixedly as if the small neat letters already on the page might provide a clue for what should follow. *How much do I tell him about the cellar?* he wondered. *Certainly not the whole story. I am too old for confession to be any help. The facts: I shall stick to the facts. They are story enough.* He resumed writing.

> Your advice to me was wise and my first install-ment comes with this letter. A rougher copy should have already arrived from the desert. I have called this scroll the *Book of Fires.* Certainly, its oracles are not unlike molten sulphur hurled down from the heavens on the heads of Yahweh's truculent people. Even now, after so many years, I feel a kind of residual heat when I read it. Jeremiah was so angry in those early days. We both made the mistake of youth, thinking that the more vitriolic our pronouncements, the more chance people would respond.

The tragedy was that it almost worked.

It was in the year Carchemish was destroyed. Nebuchadnezzar was still just a crown prince, leading the army in the name of his aging father. You would have been about fourteen and must remember something of the turmoil that seized our city. News of the carnage kept trickling into Jerusalem like the smell of a dead rodent you cannot quite find. The whole Assyrian Empire was extinguished with the ease that one blows out a bedside lamp. And worse, or better from my perspective, the Egyptian army that had marched north to support the Assyrians were routed as well. Fifty thousand of their troops killed according to the official estimates. The truth was worse. The proof of Nebuchadnezzar's absolute victory limped past our borders, scurrying back to Egypt in disarray and disgrace.

I was ecstatic. For ten years Jeremiah had been warning us about the Babylonians—Yahweh's pruning hook. But it was a preposterous assertion, especially in the early days. Babylon was a thousand miles away and in the early years, their revolt against Assyria was little more than an internal squabble. Even as they gained ground, the Assyrians were still an effective buffer. And Egypt, to whom we sent tribute, would come to our aid if ever Nebuchadnezzar threatened us. Why should Jeremiah's words have been regarded?

Overnight, it all collapsed around our smug little ears like scenery used for a play suddenly falling over, leaving us, the players, foolishly fumbling for our next line. Ezekiel, I believed that our hour had come. We had the script that fit the jumbled chaos that was our new stage. The idea of a scroll was itself a command from Yahweh.[11]

"Baruch," Jeremiah said to me, "We haven't much time. Afterwards, whatever the outcome, I want to know we did our best to warn them. In this matter I have been commanded."

"If Yahweh directs us in this," I asked, "is it because he might still change his mind?"

"I do not know," was his frank answer. "However, I have thought the same thing myself. Why commission us to prepare such a formal warning if it were not so that his people might repent?"

"What's to be done with scroll once I've finished it?"

"It needs to be proclaimed publicly at some city-wide gathering. The closer Nebuchadnezzar's army comes to our gates, the more frequent we will gather in public prayer and fasting. Some auspicious solemn assembly will present itself."

"And then you will read it?"

"Not quite," said Jeremiah, a sly grin spreading over his transparent face. "You forget that I am forbidden from entering temple property.[12] Pashur would like nothing better than to lock me up again for violating the ban."

Baruch was well aware that Pashur, the head of the temple guild, was hostile to Jeremiah. "So what is your plan?"

"Why, for you to read it for me," Jeremiah said. "You go in my place."

I still remember the flush of pride that coursed through me at that moment. In a flash I saw my future: Baruch, the hero, whose voice led the people safely back from the abyss. I saw Jeremiah, dressed regally, standing close to the throne, speaking earnestly into the king's ear. And me, I was the chief scribe—the chief executive to a now repentant and pliable king.

All these years, and I have told no one this, but I actually practised my elocution in secret. I searched for just the right cadence and tone to coax from each oracle its full potency. Like a peacock I strutted back and forth in my small room swelling up to fit the future I had created for myself. And why not? For ten years Jeremiah had suffered at the hands of everyone. Twice he had been arrested. My own career was a mess. Now at last, Yahweh would vindicate us—and himself too, of course.

It happened along the lines of Jeremiah's prescience. Nebuchadnezzar marched south along the coast of the Great Ocean[13] as far as Ashkelon.[14] He was seventy miles from us! Frightened villagers hustled into our city seeking protection. A day of fasting and prayer was announced.

"What is your plan?" asked Jeremiah, once the date was proclaimed.

"I have had a private word with Gemariah, Shaphan's son," I answered. "He has a room on the second floor of the apartments attached to the temple. He has agreed to give me access to it. I will wait for a lull in the day's agenda and speak from his window. He will position himself in the crowd, close to the apartment entrance. If Pashur sends police to arrest me, then Micaiah, Gemariah's son, will come and warn me. A passageway connects the upper level of the apartments to the palace. I can get away."

"You are not unwilling to do this favour for me?" Jeremiah asked. "It is risky."

Unwilling? I would fight anyone who stood in my way. But I grinned back at him. "Jeremiah, this might be my finest hour. You will be proud of me. Your words will pour into their ears with such eloquence that the wax of stubbornness will melt away."

"Don't be too optimistic," he replied. But he gripped both my arms and grinned just as freely back into my face. We were young. We were angry. And we wanted results so badly.

Ezekiel, I was brilliant! The angry voice of Yahweh descended on them from my second story pulpit. Their sins were paraded out in all their tawdry rags.

"Thus says Yahweh:

'How gladly would I treat you like sons and give you the most beautiful inheritance of any nation. I thought you would call me Father and not turn away from following me.[15] But like a woman unfaithful to her husband, so you have been unfaithful to me. Why should I forgive you? Your children have forsaken me and sworn by gods that are not gods. I supplied all their needs, yet they committed adultery and thronged to the houses of prostitutes. They are well-fed lusty stallions, each neighing for another man's wife.[16] You have as many gods as you have villages in Judah![17] Woe to you O Jerusalem! How long will you be unclean?[18] The prophet's prophesy lies, the priests rule by their own authority, and my people love it this way.[19]

'Even if Moses and Samuel were to stand before me,

my heart would not go out to this people. Send them away from my presence. Let them go! And if they ask you, "Where shall we go?" tell them, "This is what Yahweh says: Those destined for death, to death: those for the sword, to the sword; those for starvation, to starvation; those for captivity, to captivity.[20] I will devastate this city and make it an object of scorn; all who pass by will be appalled and will scoff because of all its wounds. I will make them eat the flesh of their sons and daughters, and they will eat one another's flesh during the stress of the siege imposed on them."[21]

Standing up and hurling down those words of retribution on the heads of the people was my finest hour and I have forgotten very little of what I spoke. At the time, I thought I spoke in shocking metaphor, but Jeremiah was simply telling us the bare truth of what awaited us all.

Micaiah came to fetch me, but it was not to warn me of impending arrest. So greatly had the people been moved by my words that I was summoned to read the scroll again for the court officials who had gathered separately within the palace.

The reformation has begun, I thought. *From the people, to the council and finally to the king.*

My second reading of the day was equally effective. I had not eaten in hours but I had no hunger. Instead, I danced on a dais of euphoria, fast-footed and furious. It was my greatest performance ever, and I had the lead part—the first player to stride out and proclaim that a new drama was about to begin. Repentance would sweep our people and the anger of Yahweh would be stayed. I could tell the courtiers had been as stirred as the people and, dare I say, convicted by my words.

After the second reading, Jeremiah and I were told to hide ourselves away while my scroll was read to the king. I went reluctantly. It was an unwarranted precaution in light of my accomplishments. The rest of that day we sat in the warehouse cellar and waited for the news. I remember fretting that my clothing was not right for an audience with the king, that my beard needed trimming and that I now smelled of sweat from the exertion of the day.

Then my father came, slowly pushing back the false floor of the warehouse that was the ceiling of our cellar cave. He descended heavily down the short ladder, gripping the sides tightly and finally faced us. His face was as grey as the light.

"King Jehoiakim has burned the scroll and mocked your oracles," he began. "Soldiers are searching the city for both of you. I have brought some food, clothing and a lamp. My servant will bring you more."

I began to retch and turned away into a corner. Nothing but a bit of bile dribbled off the end of my tongue, but my stomach kept tightening and heaving. I could not breathe and my vision blurred. Still I could not stop retching. I felt Jeremiah's hands. One hand pressed my forehead, the other encircled my chest so that most of my bent body was supported.

"We did what was asked of us," he whispered. "There is no shame in obedience."

In time, Jehoiakim forgot about us and we came out of hiding. But we were not free to move about the city completely until Jehoiakim was killed five years later.

Baruch did not add much more to the letter. He was including a scribe's writing box as a gift to Sarah. It had caught his fancy one day in the market, since it had space for five colours of ink. When it came to decorating documents, the Egyptians were unsurpassed. *It will make a useful toy if nothing else. She can dab the colours on anything and I will include some brushes instead of styli.* He found a caravan that was well guarded and made the arrangements with one of its merchants to carry his bundle to Babylon.

Now to write the next section while I wait for news that the scroll has arrived safely.

––––

Ezekiel received the package safely and dispatched a short note of receipt via the desert route. He hastily added four words after his signature. *Nebuchadnezzar marches. Have care.*

Among the Jews in Babylon, the receipt of any letter was eventful and considered, for the most part, to be communal property. Everybody had lost some family in the destruction of Jerusalem, usually parents. Though adults, they were a community of orphans. Like people who have escaped a shipwreck, Ezekiel's community kept scanning the horizon for news of who else might have escaped and floated safely onto some foreign shore. The mere fact that Baruch wrote dislodged the feeling that the Jews at Babylon were the sole survivors. They were not permanently isolated.

Ezekiel was especially glad for the letters. They gave Sarah links to her grandfather, who would otherwise have remained a vacuous name. He spread the scroll out on a table so that she could see its beauty. Scattered through the neat columns of black markings were larger coloured letters that marked the beginning of new oracles.

"They look like little coloured birds all hidden in a big black tree," said Sarah.

"I'm going to write your grandfather and tell him that his scroll arrived safely."

"Tell him I like the present he sent me. It's very fine and none of my friends has anything like it. I have already made several pictures."

"Perhaps grandfather would like one."

"I will give you one and you can send it to him in your letter."

So along with his Baruch's note, Sarah sent a small sheet on which she had drawn a picture of herself and Ezekiel standing in the public square of their compound—at least that is what she said it was. "So that he will know what we look like when he comes."

She pestered her father to ask Baruch to send more of the round coloured discs of ink.

"And tell Grandpapa to bring lots more, too, when he comes to visit us."

"Egypt is a very long way away and your grandfather is very busy. He might not be able to come," Ezekiel warned her.

"Does he make the colours?"

"He writes stories."

"What kind?"

"He writes about what happened to our homeland, to Jerusalem and the temple. He explains how they were torn down. Most of his stories are very sad. Some of them are in the scroll that he sent."

"Do you tell him about your stories?" she asked him.

"I haven't yet."

"You should. They might cheer him up. Does he know about the dancing bones?"

Ezekiel wasn't sure he had heard her right. "What do you mean?"

"The time you saw all the bones dancing—that one."

"However do you happen to know about my dancing bones?" Ezekiel asked, dumfounded.

"Oh everyone knows that story. We play a game with it."

"A game? Sarah, that was a story I told to all the grownup people when Belnuus, the elder, died. I didn't want people to be sad then. The dancing bones was a kind of picture that Yahweh put into my head before that. But Belnuus's funeral was a good time to tell people about it. It was a story for the parents."

"Yes, but everyone was there when you told it. Some of the older children heard it and my friend Lucias asked her parents to explain it."

Ezekiel knew he was a poor father at best and definitely inexperienced. He had no idea how to deal with an eight-year-old calmly informing him that one of his most vivid oracles had been converted to a child's game. *And a happy story as well,* he thought. He adopted what he hoped was a natural tone, as if what she had said was no more unusual than what had happened to one of her rag dolls.

"Sarah, what exactly is the game that you and the other children play—this dancing bone game?"

"It's like your story. First, we all get together by the big fire pit at the centre of the compound. Then somebody is picked to stay at the pit with their eyes closed and has to count to one hundred. Then while he is counting, everyone else goes to hide somewhere and pretend that we are dead. You can't move once you've hidden. We're supposed to be dead skeletons in graves."

"And then what happens?" Ezekiel prompted.

"Well, the person who's counted comes to find us. He has to carry a stick and he touches us on the head and says in a big loud voice, "come with me to Jerusalem." And we jump up and have to do a dance around him, like we're a ghost. Then we run back to the fire pit and wait for the others. The last person who's found gets to be the seeker in the next round."

"Sarah, you are right. I should tell Baruch the dancing bones story and I will also tell him about your game. They are sure to cheer him up. You can draw a picture of your game and I will include it in my next letter."

"I'm going to see mother some day," Sarah replied.

"What?"

"My mother. Shaheena. I'll see her some day."

"What makes you think of her just at this moment?" Ezekiel asked.

"That's what your bone story said. Everybody who has been put into graves and turned into skeletons will be made back into live people. And when everyone is alive again, we will all walk back to Jerusalem and live there." Sarah turned and skipped lightly through the doorway of their home, calling back to him, "I'm going to play with Lucias."

———

To Baruch who lives in the Jewish quarter at Tahpanhes, from Ezekiel among the exiles at Babylon.

Greetings. Here it is well with us. May it be well with you.

The scroll is a magnificent tribute to Jeremiah and arrived without blemish. It is kept with our other writings: the laws of Moses, the oracles of Hosea and Amos, and others. Gradually we are finding our old writings but they come from the oddest sources. The scroll is a solemn reminder that Yahweh is a God who speaks in great detail and that what he speaks comes to pass—for good or ill.

I am greatly blessed here for we cling more tightly to Yahweh worship and traditions than ever before. There is great relief that the punishment is over, that all the words of judgement have come to pass. Even I have been released from the terrible visions that used to seize me.

I am no longer feared by the children, who used to run
and find their mothers if I came too close to where they
played. Those were terrible days for me, yet I could not
escape them.

It puzzles me that the same events could instigate
such opposite responses. You are among Jews who now
follow Ishtar, and I am among Jews who wait in great
simplicity for the kindness of Yahweh to begin.

Sarah has instructed me to tell you some of my
"happy stories" so that you would be cheered. I did receive
a vision of hope. Little does she realize that it came from
her. Belnuus, a much-loved elder, died here in Babylon
and I presided over his burial. I chose his death as the time
to proclaim an oracle given me some time earlier.

It was a vision of a huge valley full of dry bones—
piles of skulls and ribs.[22] It was like the earth covering a
mass grave had blown away, revealing its occupants, who
had been heaped on top of each other by the thousands.
Then in my vision, I watched and the bones came together
and flesh, even clothing, covered them. They did not stir.
Then my guide in the vision said to me, "Breathe over
them, that they will live." And as I breathed, they moved,
getting up and walking around, hugging and greeting
each other.

The whole valley was alive and as I watched, my
guide said to me again, "These are the scattered people
of Yahweh, who will be brought back to live in their own
land. Yahweh will make a covenant of peace with them.
It will be an everlasting covenant. I will be their God and
they will be my people. My dwelling place will be among
them forever."[23]

The funeral of an elder was a natural public forum to
make known the vision and its meaning. Yahweh blessed
me with a ministry of hope for a people whose bones are
dried up and whose hope is gone.[24] But I was astonished to
learn that Sarah and her friends have taken my vision and
made a game of it! They call it their dancing bones game,
a kind of hide and seek that ends in all the players returning to their home base, which they call Jerusalem.

In their innocence they have grasped the essential

truth better than most of us—a dead people resurrected and returned to our homeland. She tells me with great certainty that at Jerusalem she will see Shaheena again. Who am I to say she is wrong?

She asks when you will come to us. I will not ask the same, only assure you that you would be welcomed beyond words. Only you know what is best and I would understand if you chose to be buried in the same soil as your friend, just as I will be buried here in Babylon.

BY MY OWN HAND, EZEKIEL

Sarah asks most respectfully for more discs of paint to be included in your next packet. Another of her pictures is with this letter.

TO EZEKIEL, A PRIEST AMONG THE EXILES IN BABYLON, LIVING BY THE KEDAR RIVER, FROM BARUCH, A SCRIBE AMONG THE JEWS AT TAHPANHES IN EGYPT:

I hasten to respond. With this letter comes another scroll I have copied out. There are also enough discs of coloured ink to make Sarah happy for many months. What a delight Yahweh has given you and, through news of her, to me also.

Your warning that Nebuchadnezzar advances was propitious. But I do not fear too bloody an engagement should he march this far. My news is that Hophra has been executed and his former loyal commander, General Amasis, is now king of all Egypt.

Exactly how this coup was accomplished I have no details and there is an uneasiness even here at Tahpanhes. Johanan tells me that Amasis is still consolidating his support. There are pockets of resistance. I judge that to mean he is quite vulnerable to invasion. Jeremiah promised Nebuchadnezzar would come and depart unscathed.[25]

Imagine the irony if Nebuchadnezzar managed to kill us Jews who fled from him before. A frontier city such as ours is an obvious target. For now, we wait. There is nothing else we can do and nowhere else to run.

The scroll is called *The Book of Consolation*.[26] It was never circulated in Jerusalem, and certainly it is not meant for the people who live here. But I sense that its time of proclamation has arrived. The oracles it contains did not come to Jeremiah all at once. Some I think he composed in the early days, when King Josiah was still alive and Jeremiah lived in his home village of Anathoth. Those were more hopeful days for us, yet he kept them to himself. Not until close to the end, after Nebuchadnezzar had begun the siege, did we even establish them as a formal collection.

Jeremiah's lot was mostly pain and humiliation. But somehow, Yahweh's spirit rested on him—no, it was more than that: it dwelt within him. And I, intimate though I was, could only be an onlooker—the cryptic cipher, pen always ready to capture the holy points of intersection where two worlds touched.

There is one brilliant couplet within the scroll of Consolation. When you read it aloud it will be like manna itself come back down to feed you. It is like your happy image of dry bones dancing:

"The time will come when I will write my law on the hearts of every man and from the least to the greatest they will all know me. For I will forgive their wickedness, and remember their sins no more."

For Jeremiah that was prophecy already present in his life. He could not have survived otherwise. But me, I only got to touch the words, not apprehend them. And now to send them out to you from my jar in which I've kept them hidden, like seeds I hoped would grow, leaves me feeling as if I have announced a great family feast knowing I cannot attend.

I feel like a slave consort hired to give birth for a wife who was barren—as Hagar did with Abraham. The scroll is not my own, its family is in Babylon and I must relinquish it. Yet a small part of me dies with each letter that I send you. The truth is, I am living where I belong, among the followers of Ishtar, among those who have deserted Yahweh. Oh, rest assured I do not go to her temple. But I too was a worshipper of foreign gods. And for my sins I have been branded with my own peculiar mark of Cain, which does not kill me outright as I deserve, but remains like an open wound that will not heal.

You said once that I do not lose sight of truth. Well, it is time you know the whole truth about me.

Ambition. That was the secret altar that I visited each day. Some would say it was not such a secret. I wrote you earlier about living in the cellar, hiding from Jehoiakim. What I did not tell you then was that it was in the cellar that Yahweh spoke to me.

It was the only time Yahweh ever noticed me. The oracle did not come to me directly. Jeremiah was the intermediary and I know he meant the words kindly enough.

It was evening, not that it mattered, for down there the light was all the same. My father had brought wine and I was drinking hard.

"You are greatly burdened," Jeremiah said. "My troubles have spilled into your life and I am sorry."

"It's not your fault. Yahweh presses you into his purposes."

"The fault is his, then." Jeremiah spoke without feeling.

"Yes," I said, exhaling anger. "Since you are the first to utter the unspeakable and raise a protest, I will add to it. It is Yahweh who harasses me. His words, which I have so faithfully copied, have brought me low." I snorted and Jeremiah laughed.

"Yes, I see your point. How much lower could we be than in a cellar? You think Yahweh is unjust, that the faithful should always be rewarded?"

I said nothing, and Jeremiah spoke again. "Baruch, if Yahweh were truly just, which one of us would be left alive at the end of all that's going to happen?"

Still, I said nothing. What could I say? He pressed on.

"Yahweh has noticed your thoughts and is not pleased." My whole body went numb as if I was drinking a tincture of opium instead of wine. "Yahweh knows I exist?"

"Did you think he is so aloof that he does not know each of us, as if the contents of one man's heart is too small a thing for him to notice? I do not think so. You are too educated, and already you have seen too much. No, I will tell you what you hoped for under that zealous mask of righteousness you keep glued to your face. You thought Yahweh would overlook the grand ambitions you keep as fantasies for yourself."

"Is it a sin to have hopes?" I asked sullenly

"Sometimes it is."

"And in my case?"

"In your case this is what Yahweh says to you. Yes, Baruch, an oracle that needs no further proclamation than this putrid dungeon, for to you alone it is sent. Thus says Yahweh. I will bring disaster on all who live in this land. Should you seek great things for yourself? Seek them not. Instead, be content with the mercy it pleases me to give you. For wherever you go, I will let you escape with your life."[27]

And so, Ezekiel, I who was not even repentant was given my life. Why me? Oh, the easy answer is that Yahweh protected me to do the bidding of Jeremiah—a necessary factotum so that his words might be preserved. But that is too easy. Yahweh needing Baruch to accomplish his purposes? Not even my ego could support that supposition. But all these years, each time I saw someone die, especially one of the faithful, I would wish it could be me. Grace has dogged me ever since the cellar, and I cannot escape. Yahweh remains unjust for he lets me live when I am no more fit than anyone else.

By my own hand, Baruch

———

Nebuchadnezzar arrived in Tahpanhes, stayed just long enough to tear down the gates of the garrison fort, scatter the small defending regiment and dash on. His goal was a city called Heliopolis, home to a magnificent temple built for the worship of Re, the Sun god.[28]

"He is not here to occupy, only to intimidate," explained Johanan to Baruch.

"It is an ancient strategy: humiliate a people's gods and you humiliate them. It proves that your gods are superior," replied Baruch.

"Like the Yahweh temple?" asked Johanan pointedly.

"Do the diviners of Re predict their demise because Re himself ordains it? I had not heard that," answered Baruch. "But of course, you always get better news than I do."

Johanan replied, "I do not believe we have seen the last of the Babylonians."

"Why?"

"Nebuchadnezzar's troops were an attack regiment—well armed, well mounted and able to move fast."

"Your point?" said Baruch testily.

"Booty. The spoils of conquest. They can't take the time to properly ransack the temples, much less carry the loot with them. Yet without it, where's the proof of their victory? No, I fully expect we'll see a second battalion and they'll look more like caravaners from the huge wagons they'll drive. I watched them strip Jerusalem so that all that was left was bones. They've done it hundreds of times. They have an engineering corps who are specially trained."

"I see what you mean. You'd best be careful how close you get to them. No doubt they'll press anybody they can into service." Baruch knew that Johanan would go and watch. The soldier within him demanded it.

———

Nebuzaradan rode at the front of the slowly moving train of carts. He was sixty-five, too old for the assault corps that had ridden this way a week earlier. Still, he was fit enough to campaign with his old friend and commander, King Nebuchadnezzar. Together, they'd tramped up and down the Fertile Crescent, been to the ends of the world and beyond. They hadn't always won, but they'd also never definitively lost. Egypt had always eluded them. But twice before they almost got there. *And now that I'm finally here, I have no more time than to pack up the spoils and march all the way back home again.*

The men under his command knew their jobs well. They would set up closest to the largest temple. Within an hour of arriving, a portable smelter would be assembled and huge mounds of fuel would be scavenged. The town perimeter would be made secure and sentries posted. Then a highly trained group of artisans would be escorted through each area. It was their job to identify and select the objects to be shipped intact, destined to go on display in Babylon as proof of Nebuchadnezzar's foreign conquest. It was the same procedure for every city they had conquered. Only the truly unusual would be kept in its original state. Thirty years of collecting war trophies had raised Nebuchadnezzar's artistic standards considerably. They hadn't really found much worth keeping since Jerusalem.

Now that was a city that had style, he thought. *Those gold encased pillars we took from their temple—it took two wagons and eight horses each to drag them back to Babylon. It was worth it though. They must have been five hundred years old, and the goldsmithing—incredible— their whole tops looked like a palm tree with fruit.[29] I was sure they'd get broken before we got them home.*

Anything the curators did not reserve would be either smashed, burned or melted into large ingots for easy transport. Already the bronze overlay was being peeled away from the walls and pillars of the temple. The first bars of metal would be cooling in their moulds before the day was out.

Nebuzaradan was thorough in this job, as he had been in all the other duties of war he'd been assigned. *This is the booty that finances our armies. Without it, how could we go home?*

He gazed around at the civilians who, once it was clear they would not be harmed, stood in distant clumps. *They are not all Egyptians,* he thought. *Where have I seen people like them before?* He spurred his horse forward to approach some of them. He was curious. It was a trait that encouraged longevity.

————

"Baruch." Johanan was breathing heavily. "Baruch, you've got to come—quick."

"What's wrong?" Johanan's pale face bespoke of something serious.

"A Babylonian officer, the one who's in charge—he has found out that there are Jews living here. He is making inquiries about Jeremiah. I did not know exactly what to say. He is insistent in his questions."

Afraid he'd run you through if you told him, Baruch thought. Baruch was certain he knew who was asking questions. Baruch had been with Jeremiah at Jerusalem. There was only one Babylonian who would be asking about Jeremiah. He looked closely at Johanan. *He's also afraid I'll betray him, tell the Babylonian just who was responsible for bringing Jeremiah down here to die in obscurity. Johanan probably has no idea that Jeremiah was offered a court position by Nebuchadnezzar.*[30] A wonderful power coursed through him. He had never before held another man's life in his mouth. *Just one short sentence, and I can have Johanan killed.*

Baruch spent his hour-long walk to the city centre immersed in a delicious fantasy: Johanan and all the other vermin were being savagely punished by the Babylonians. The details of it shifted in time with his feet but the plot was as steady as his gait. Sometimes they would be killed outright—run through their stomachs with swords so that they would fall heavily to the ground, hands clutching their fronts, trying to keep their viscera from spilling out. It was a gruesome way to die. Sometimes they would not die, but instead be stripped and tied together, destined for harsh service somewhere within Nebuchadnezzar's empire. He thought of Inanna, Johanan's wife, who was ostensibly a novitiate within the temple guild of Ishtar, the goddess of love. *Now the soldiers will use her for what she is.* He imagined her spread out over some table, surrounded by callused soldiers jostling each other for a chance at her. Her usual look of insolent superiority was replaced by a mixture of shock and shame.

Not since the days in the cellar had Baruch been seized by such anger. The opportunity for revenge filled him, as if some potent anodyne now pumped through his body in place of blood. *Not revenge, it is justice, and it will be my words that bring them low.*

Baruch pictured himself standing beside the Babylonian commander watching the punishments that paraded through his mind. *I will blame Gedaliah's murder on them,* he thought. *I will implicate them, and the very fact that they fled here to Egypt, hoping to escape reprisal, will prove their guilt.* Baruch's head pounded with the elixir of retribution. His lifetime of losing, rejection and derision had found an opening through which to vent. Like the high waters behind a dam, exploiting a small crack, Baruch's fantasies eroded the dyke of restraint he had lived behind most of his life. *This rag-tag bunch of Jews thought they could escape Yahweh? They thought Jeremiah was an empty headed fanatic and me, his feckless amanuensis? Now they will see who comes out on top.*

The force of the fantasy carried Baruch effortlessly to where the Babylonians looters had set up camp. Baruch recognized their leader at once. Nebuzaradan's face bore a long ugly scar starting close to one eye and ending just under his chin. Baruch remembered it vividly from when they had met at Jerusalem. Baruch approached and coughed politely.

"Commander Nebuzaradan?"

"What of it?" Nebuzaradan looked at the tiny, bald man who stood squarely in front of him.

"I am Baruch ben Neriah of Jerusalem, the servant of Jeremiah to whom you showed kindness."

"Yes, I remember you now. You are his scribe. I made inquiries when we were close to Jerusalem. They told me that a company of Jews fled to Egypt after Gedaliah was murdered. Rumour was that Jeremiah was among them. Since you are here, I see it is true. Is he with you?"

"Alas, no. He has been dead now almost three years."

"Killed?"

"No, he never fully recovered from the hardships of our city's siege."

"He should have come back to Babylon. Nebuchadnezzar set great stock in his oracles. They have all proved most accurate." Nebuzaradan allowed himself a tight-lipped grin, which Baruch mimicked. "What brought Jeremiah to Egypt?" The question was casually put.

This is it, thought Baruch. *Johanan and all the others are mine to deliver up. The do not follow Yahweh. They deserve to die.*

Speak, part of him raged. *This is your hour.* An intense pressure filled his head so that black spots clouded his vision. His tongue grew large, or his throat small—he wasn't sure and it didn't matter. He was choking. His insides detached from their skin shell and boiled furiously like stew in a caldron. He felt his bowels dissolving in the boiling pottage that now defined him.. He felt hot urine soak the front of his robe and splash the ground.

"I said, how came Jeremiah to Egypt?" Nebuzaradan repeated.

A voice answered and Baruch, though he uttered the sounds, listened to it as though it was another's, expectantly awaiting what would come out. "He came as a consequence of a powerful oracle," he said. Baruch looked down at the front of his robe. It was dry. His tongue no longer filled his entire mouth. his bowels quieted. Yet something had departed from him. Some deep pocket of bile, hidden and festering all his life, was now lanced.A lifetime of puss and poison had spilled.

Nebuzaradan grunted. "That god he served was powerfully strange. What was his name, Yiway?"

"Yahweh," Baruch corrected weakly. "And yes, he is both powerful and strange."

"We never found his image. I was surprised—only a small room at the centre of his temple and a gold covered box."

"He has no images. It is a prohibition imposed on us since the beginning. Since Egypt." Baruch gave a small laugh at the irony of what he had not meant.

"Just as well, I suppose," answered Nebuzaradan. "We would have smashed it, just like we're doing here." He pointed to where three men were tying ropes to a tall willowy statue that still stood at what once was the centre of the temple. It was an elegant sculpture, set on a rounded slab of stone. The figure was a woman, naked, with ram's horns extending in symmetrical loops from her forehead. One hand was raised high as if bestowing a blessing. The other hung down at her side and held a short sword. The entire statue was sheathed in beaten gold.

"Whose temple are we razing?" asked Nebuzaradan.

"Her name is Ishtar," said Baruch. "The Queen of the Heaven."

"Not any longer," grunted Nebuzaradan laconically. "By the end of the year she'll be just so many gold coins in our commissary's treasury. The year after that, she'll be pay in the hands of our troops."

"The privileges of the victor," said Baruch. "Coins of fertility."

But Nebuzaradan did not respond. Instead, he returned to a topic Baruch had hoped was now forgotten. "What kind of oracle caused Jeremiah to come all this way?"

"His God—our God—Yahweh gave him a vision that Egypt would be punished. May it please Nebuchadnezzar to learn that Jeremiah foretold his arrival, here, on this very ground."

"Just as it happened at Jerusalem," murmured Nebuzaradan. He stared intently at Baruch.

"How many other nations does your god intend to deliver into our hands?"

Baruch gave a giddy laugh. "I did not know that there were any left standing against you."

"But your master, Jeremiah, pronounced oracles against other nations—yes?"

"Yes."

"How many?"

"About ten nations, I think."

"And you have records of these prophecies?" pressed the general.

"Of some, not all," lied Baruch.

"But you have a recollection of them. You could write down their essential parts in pleasing cadence? You are a scribe, after all."

"Yes," Baruch answered. *What trap is being laid for me?*

A slow grin spread across Nebuzaradan's face. The scar did not move in sync with the rest of his features so that it looked more like a lopsided leer than a smile. "It would give Nebuchadnezzar entertainment to hear these oracles as you call them—especially the ones about Egypt."

Baruch said nothing. Nebuzaradan continued speaking, looking all the while into Baruch's face. "But there are some that he should not hear, I think. Am I not right?"

"Not all the words of Jeremiah would please your king," replied Baruch.

"I did not think so. It is why, I think, that Jeremiah did not come with me the first time. He would not have held his tongue even in our throne room. But you, on the other hand, are free to pick your words with great prudence. You are now simply an historian."

"It is true. Yahweh spoke only to Jeremiah. I had no such insights."

"We treat Jews well in our lands. Their ghetto thrives, and your king—the one we took hostage—still lives comfortably at court."

"So I have heard," replied Baruch. "We send and receive letters from time to time. Nebuchadnezzar is gracious to those he has conquered." Baruch knew what was coming, but was determined to wait for it.

"Tell me, Baruch, what detains you here in Egypt?"

"Nothing."

"As I thought. Jeremiah is dead, but you will come with us. Nebuchadnezzar might find you vastly more interesting than any other booty we might haul back. You will make yourself available for the entertainment of Nebuchadnezzar, but you may live where you wish."

"But the other Jews, the ones who came with Jeremiah?"

Nebuzaradan shrugged. "I have only need for one man to recite the words of Jeremiah, not a choir. They can shift for themselves here. We leave in two days time. Be here at sunrise."

Baruch bowed solemnly and turned to go.

"And do not try to run," added Nebuzaradan to Baruch's retreating back.

Run? He thought. For the first time in my life there is nothing chasing me.

Epilogue

History confirms the continuing esteem accorded to Baruch for his faithfulness to Jeremiah—both to the man and to the preservation of his oracles. Indeed, many scholars believe that Baruch wrote the narrative portions of Jeremiah's book. The reverence with which Baruch was regarded continued for hundreds of years. Three other books, all written much later, are attributed to him, including the *Book of Baruch*, contained in the Apocrypha. These deliberate attributions are most properly interpreted as ongoing homage to the man's singular contribution to the editing and preserving of holy writings.

Nothing can be verified concerning Baruch's last days. According to the Jewish historian Josephus (75 AD), Baruch did indeed return from Egypt to Babylon to prepare the hearts of the exiles for their eventual return to Jerusalem. If this tradition is accurate, then it would have been children like Sarah whom he instructed.

Endnotes

[1] Jeremiah 43:8. Jeremiah took large (pavement) stones and buried them in the entrance of the royal palace at Tahpanhes. He then prophesied that Nebuchadnezzar would come and place his throne on top of the stones. To the extent that the Egyptian authorities knew Jeremiah, his various public prophecies against them would not have made the refugees very welcome.

[2] Most scholars agree that the first deportation of Jews occurred in 598 BC, about eleven years before the final destruction of Jerusalem. Jerusalem fell in 587, after a three-year siege. It is logical to assume that Jeremiah lived at least five years in Egypt although no details of his death are known for certain. If Baruch is writing shortly after Jeremiah dies, he would be writing in about 582. This dating assumes that the murder of Gedaliah occurred very shortly after the fall of Jerusalem.

[3] Jeremiah 36 contains the story of how Jeremiah's scroll was burned. King Jehoiakim was the son of Josiah and ruled from 609-598 BC.

[4] Jeremiah chapters 46-51 contains oracles of judgment against other nations. Egypt and Babylon receive the most attention but eight other lesser kingdoms are judged. On the basis of content, they were composed by Jeremiah throughout his lifetime. Early editors of his book chose to group them together, almost as an appendix to the main story.

[5] Jeremiah 17:1

[6] Jeremiah 51:59 confirms that Zedekiah went to Babylon. Jeremiah 27:2ff speaks of the meeting of five nation states at Jerusalem.

[7] Jeremiah 51:64

[8] Jeremiah 39:6, also II Kings 52:18

[9] Jeremiah 29:29. Zephaniah was a senior priest at Jerusalem and sought to protect Jeremiah from various accusations. In Jeremiah 52:24 he is recorded among those who were executed by Nebuchadnezzar.

[10] Jeremiah 36:26

[11] Jeremiah 36:1

[12] Jeremiah 36:5. Pashur, while unsuccessful in having Jeremiah found guilty of treason, was able to bar him from temple property.

[13] The Mediterranean. Carchemish was a substantial city located on the Euphrates River, close to the modern-day Turkey/Syrian border. The Assyrians had retreated from the western arm of the Fertile Crescent ten years earlier, and the Egyptians controlled the area through a variety of garrison towns. Nebuchadnezzar had steadily pressured the Assyrians from the east so that by 605, all remaining

Assyrian troops were massed around Carchemish. Their destruction at Carchemish marked the end of the Assyrian Empire, a civilization that endured 400 years.

[14] A Philistine sea-coast city situated south of Jerusalem. Nebuchadnezzar would probably have campaigned south all the way to Egypt except that the sudden death of his father required him to return to Babylon in great haste and secure the throne. As it was, Jehoiakim was forced to switch alliances and began to grudgingly send tribute to Babylon instead of Egypt.

[15] Jeremiah 3:19,20

[16] Jeremiah 5:7,8

[17] Jeremiah 11:13

[18] Jeremiah 13:26,27

[19] Jeremiah 5:31

[20] Jeremiah 15:1,2

[21] Jeremiah 19:8,9

[22] The complete vision is recorded in Ezekiel 37.

[23] Ezekiel 37:26ff

[24] Ezekiel 37:11

[25] Jeremiah 43:12

[26] Jeremiah 30-31 forms a discrete collection of poetry, all offering consolation and hope that at some future time, Yahweh will bring about great salvation for his people.

[27] This oracle directed to Baruch is located in Jeremiah 45. The chapter is five verses in length and is dated as occurring immediately after King Jehoiakim burned Jeremiah's scroll. It is conspicuously misplaced within the overall book, suggesting some reluctance on the part of the editor, probably Baruch, to admit to its existence.

[28] Jeremiah 43:8-13 contains a prophecy that Nebuchadnezzar would invade Egypt, demolish the sacred pillars in the temple of the Sun—that is, the temple of Re, Egypt's chief god. Nebuchadnezzar would depart with great booty and without harm. Historical records of Nebuchadnezzar's campaign against Egypt are incomplete. He definitely invaded Egypt in 567 BC. The major temple of Re was at Heliopolis, located about five miles from modern day Cairo. The temple approach included two rows of obelisks through which people advanced to the temple entrance. One of these still stands. Scholarly consensus is that Jeremiah's oracle refers to this particular temple. Yet Jeremiah's earlier oracle, if taken literally, also promised that Nebuchadnezzar would visit Tahpanhes. Nebuchadnezzar died in 562. There is no evidence that he occupied Egypt but neither did Egypt seek to

expand her natural borders. A cordial peace seems to have prevailed between the two major world powers.

[29] II Chronicles 3:15ff. The two pillars commissioned by King Solomon were so outstanding that each one was individually named: Jakin and Boaz. They were capped with an elaborate array of gold chains and cornice work extending eight feet in diameter. From the chains hung 100 pomegranates, giving the effect of huge trees, heavy with fruit. Two hundred years earlier Hezekiah, then king of Judah, entertained certain envoys from the city of Babylon (II Kings 20:12ff). In the course of his hospitality, he displayed all the wealth of the city. The prophet Isaiah, on hearing the news, foretold that everything the Babylonians had seen would someday be taken as booty back to their own city.

[30] Jeremiah 40:4

Printed in the United States
29847LVS00004B/338